C000283539

For my old mate Neil Scott

ed 2010

Press
imscombe Port
cestershire, GL5 2QG
orypress.co.uk

yton, 2010

David Clayton to be identified as the Author
has been asserted in accordance with the
Designs and Patents Act 1988.

erved. No part of this book may be reprinted
d or utilised in any form or by any electronic,
r other means, now known or hereafter invented,
otocopying and recording, or in any information
rieval system, without the permission in writing
lishers.

ry Cataloguing in Publication Data.
ecord for this book is available from the British Library.

24 5876 2

nd origination by The History Press
reat Britain

THE
PRES
NORTH
MISCELL

DAVID CL

First publis

The Histo
The Mill,
Stroud, Gl
www.theh

© David C

The right
of this wor
Copyrights

All rights r
or reprodu
mechanica
including
storage or
from the P

British Lib
A catalogu

ISBN 978 0

Typesetting
Printed in

The
Hist
Pres

AUTHOR'S ACKNOWLEDGEMENTS

Any work on Preston North End Football Club is going to be steeped in history and this book is no different. Of course, being a miscellany, it's packed with snippets rather than lengthy essays – for that is the nature of the beast (not Jon Parkin). I've tried to uncover as many facts I think may be of interest to PNE fans as I can and present them informally and, hopefully, in a readable and entertaining format – if you think I have by the time you read the last page, I've done my job. There are plenty of stats, too, with some fascinating records recounted in the following pages as well as plenty of vignettes on the events and people who have contributed to this great club's history.

In the research and writing of this book, I'd like to thank former Lilywhites player and boss Les Chapman for writing the foreword for me. Thanks also to Will Unwin, Alex Rowen, Ian Rigby and Mike Payne. I'd also like to thank Michelle Tilling at The History Press for all her patience – particularly her patience! – support and encouragement. I hope you enjoy *The Preston North End Miscellany* and maybe find out one of two things you didn't know about this grand old club.

David Clayton, 2010

INTRODUCTION

There are sleeping giants and then there is Preston North End. This club did more in its early years than almost any other, but modern times have been lean to say the least. Eight failed play-off attempts tell their own story but one day, the Lilywhites will rise again and return to the top division where they belong. Let's face it, any side that can boast Tom Finney and Bill Shankly among its former players must be a bit special. . . .

FOREWORD

By former North End player and manager

Les Chapman

I arrived at Deepdale in 1986 as player/assistant manager working alongside the charismatic John McGrath. I was soon aware of a massive expectancy at the club because of the history and tradition and, of course, having arguably the best player in the world of his generation in the shape of Sir Tom Finney, who I had the pleasure of meeting on numerous occasions.

We had a great start and eventually gained promotion in the first season. I can honestly say that I enjoyed my playing days at Preston as much as anywhere I've played throughout my career. After spells at Oldham (twice), Huddersfield, Bradford, Rochdale, Stockport (twice) and San José Earthquakes, that's a fair indictment of the esteem I hold Preston North End in. I finished my playing career with the Lilywhites and unfortunately only scored one goal – but it did happened to be the winner at Leyton Orient which secured promotion for us! It's the quality, not the quantity!

We had a great mix of experience and youth in the team, with the likes of Frank Worthington, John Thomas, Sam Allardyce, Osher Williams, Bob Atkins and others, and not only were we successful we had a great team spirit and a lot of fun! When you have big characters in the dressing room you are guaranteed a daily dose of levity and adventure.

The manager himself was a larger than life character and what he lacked in academic acumen he more than made up for in his humour and knowledge of the game – he may have had trouble with his spelling, but he could tie even the sharpest of directors up in knots when it came to talking football.

Most of the nicknames of the players at that time were derived from how John wrote out their names for a training session; for instance Gary Brazil was 'Barzil,' Bob Atkins was 'Akins' and so on – you can imagine how he struggled with Ronnie Hildersley!

Anyway, as time went by the inevitable happened – John left the club and I took over. What a difference that made to my life. It's a job of incredible extremes: when you're winning it's the best job in the world, but when you lose, it's the worst. I don't know whether being close to the players as a player helped or hindered – maybe it is a bit of both, I suppose.

It was a great experience, though, and opened up other avenues for me. I left in 1992 to join Manchester City, where I still work to this day but I can honestly say the Preston North End experience was an eventful and enjoyable one!

Les Chapman, 2010

ONLY ONE LAWRO

Tommy Lawrenson, father of BBC *Match of the Day* pundit Mark, played for North End between 1949 and 1955 – but managed just one appearance in all that time. A stalwart of the reserve team during his spell at the club, Tommy was always on the fringes of the side, but never quite made the kind of impression he hoped to.

SAFE GROUND

Deepdale is the oldest continually used football ground in the world. PNE are one of just a handful of clubs to play at the stadium they initially began at.

STATUESQUE SIR TOM

Unveiled in 2004, the statue of Sir Tom Finney sits proudly outside Deepdale. It was inspired by a photograph taken during a match between North End and Chelsea at Stamford Bridge in 1956 when the great man was pictured in a pool of water during a sodden encounter. Sculpted by Sardarjee Om Puri, the monument pays tribute to the player and that watery moment.

NO-ONE LIKES THEM – WE DON'T CARE

Scoring goals for fun and racing out of the blocks for the 1930/31 campaign, North End recorded their record aggregate league away win on 4 October. Though a trip to Cold Blow Lane (says it all, really) was never considered for the annual book of 'Happy Days on the Road', Preston needed to continue their bright form and leave Millwall with both points. It was a game that ebbed and flowed, with the visitors 3–2 up at the break – having now been involved in 40 goals either way from their opening eight-and-a-half games, few expected there would be no further scoring – and they were right. The Lilywhites led 7–3 with five minutes left, but the spirited Lions pulled a couple more back before full-time to make it Millwall 5, North End 7 – a remarkable game. The hosts had their revenge later in the campaign, winning 3–1 at Deepdale and the following season won 4–1 at The Den.

OUR MAN FLINT?

England all-rounder and cricket legend Freddie Flintoff began life as a North End fan. As a child, he attended Deepdale regularly, but as his cricket career took off, he drifted away from football and has now adopted Manchester City as his team of choice. He admits he'll always have a soft spot for the Lilywhites, however, and always looks for the club's results.

SLIMFAST SIMON

Former Barnsley boss Simon Davey, a PNE player between 1995 and 1998, contracted food poisoning during his first season at Deepdale. Now manager at Hereford, the illness caused Davey to lose 17lbs in the space of week – something Simon, who has piled those lost pounds back on in recent years, would probably welcome today. . .

BOYS IN BLUE 0, BOYS IN WHITE 1

When North End agreed to take on Preston Police in February 1912, the footballers won by 22 – but it was points, not goals, as the game in question was a billiards challenge rather than a footy match.

SNATCH OF THE DAY

Gary Lineker once scored a goal for Preston during a 1–1 draw with Leicester City in November 1979. Sadly, the future England man and *Match of the Day* presenter was in Leicester colours when he put through his own goal. Ah, well. . .

BOOK EARLY!

Season 1979/80 was the first North End wore shirt sponsorship. The deal was with Pontins, the UK holiday giant famed for corny TV ads in the 1970s. If not the glamour deal some fans had been hoping for, it at least showed the club were forward-thinking, being one of only four clubs in the country to have struck a shirt deal.

THE LAST LION

David Nugent's one and only England cap in 2007 was the last time a North Ender played for England. Nugent scored a 93rd-minute goal against Andorra in Barcelona to mark his debut in style, but has never played for his country again. Prior to that, the last England player North End had was Tommy Thompson way back in 1957. He won just one cap (is there a pattern forming here?). Tom Finney won 76 caps while at Deepdale and is unlikely to be overtaken any time soon. Finney won his first cap in 1946 and his last 12 years later in 1958. In fact, no other North End player has even reached double figures for England, with Fred Dewhurst managing 9 – plus 11 goals – between 1886 and 1889.

PLAYER OF THE YEAR

Season 1967/68 was the first year the club awarded a Player of the Year Trophy and Alan Kelly was the inaugural proud recipient of the honour. Kelly notched up 44 appearances during the campaign, though he never found his way on to the score sheet.

WHAT'S UP, DOC?

Former North End player and ex-Manchester United boss Tommy Docherty proved the old adage 'you can never go back' to be true when he returned to Deepdale to take the reins for the start of the 1981/82 season. With the club celebrating its centenary season (a year late according to some historians), hopes were high that the Doc could perhaps inspire the Lilywhites to promotion, but by December and with just 17 league games played, Docherty was shown the door with his negative style driving fans away as the goals and entertainment dried up.

WEEPING WILLOWS

North End bade a fond farewell to their old training ground in 1982 when they quit Willow Farm to move to new premises between Preston and Grimsargh.

TWO PLACES AT ONCE?

The Lilywhites played two friendlies at the same time on the same day in September 1911. Whether or not they'd double-booked and felt obliged to play both games is not known, but the squads, diluted or not, won both, beating Chorley 2–0 and Merthyr Town 4–1.

COMMON KNOWLEDGE

Alf Common graced Deepdale for a short time during his distinguished career. The former England, Sunderland and Middlesbrough forward arrived part-way through the 1912/13 season and helped inspire North End to the Second Division title. Common was the first English footballer to be transferred for £1,000 when he joined Boro in 1905. PNE purchased him for slightly less, paying £250, and Common played 35 times and scored 8 goals before retiring in 1914.

BEEFY BOTHER

When the Lilywhites travelled to the Old Showground to take on Scunthorpe United two days after Christmas 1983, the players didn't know whether to wear shin pads or cricket pads when they learned legendary England cricket all-rounder Ian Botham was named in the starting XI. Playing at centre-half, 'Beefy' was marking North End striker Steve Elliott but instead of being bowled over, Elliott – in cricket terms – hit Botham all over the park as he scored a hat-trick during a 5–1 win for the vistors.

PNE ORIGINS

Preston North End may have been associated with football for over a century, but the original traces of the Lancashire side can be traced as far back as 1863, when the club was initially founded as a cricket team. Originally named Preston Nelson, the club underwent a name change in the 1860s and was relabelled Preston North End. This change was based simply on the fact that the club played their matches in northern Preston. In August 1867, the cricket side began to struggle financially and a number of new members joined the club – future Chairman William Sudell was one such member. Despite the club's deepening financial crisis, Preston risked their future by taking a lease out on Deepdale Farm in January 1875. This was, however, to prove the first step in creating Preston North End FC and the club introduced football and rugby to the farm as a means of generating new income. The PNE rugby team couldn't compete with its more established local rivals and it took only two years before the club decided to scrap their involvement in the sport and focus solely on association football.

Having played their first game against Eagley in October 1878, Preston North End FC was fast on its way to being founded and in 1880 the club was officially established. The club was to be led by a 'sporting panel' which included local businessman Major William Sudell. Sudell had noted the accomplishments of rival amateur clubs and was sure that success in football would eventually result in financial stability and so went about recruiting the best local talent, as well as a number of players from north of the border. In 1883, many names moved from Scotland to Deepdale on the promise that they would receive jobs and be paid well for their involvement with the club. This approach led to accusations of 'professionalism' and in 1885 the FA expelled PNE from the FA Cup for fielding a professional side in the amateur game. A number of clubs criticised this decision and threatened to break away and create their own league, believing professional football to be 'the way forward'. In order to combat a potential club revolt, an FA sub-committee – which included Sudell – was established. In

July 1885, the payment of players became legalised and the professional game was born.

As an original founder member of the Football League, Preston North End was established as a professional football side in 1888 and went on to dominate the league for two years. Their first ever professional team, now known as 'The Invincibles', won the league without defeat and the FA Cup without conceding a goal. A year later, the Lilywhites won their second consecutive title. Thanks to the investment of Sudell, PNE soon established themselves as a major force in English football and in 1893 the PNEFC limited company was created.

DREAM SCENARIO

Imagine if North End could confirm the title at home by beating Blackpool on the last day of the season? Oh, and throw in the Seasiders being relegated, just for good measure? Well, that's exactly what happened on 26 April 1913 – sort of. The title was definitely Preston's thanks to nearest challengers Burnley's midweek failure to beat Barnsley. Blackpool arrived already demoted from the Second Division, but didn't want to be at Deepdale with the home fans gearing up to celebrate, so they didn't make life easy, but the hosts still won 2–1. Those were the days.

DON'T GO THE MANCUNIAN WAY ...!

With Tommy Docherty, Bobby Charlton and Nobby Stiles all taking the hot-seat at Deepdale in the space of a decade, it was Manchester City's turn in 1985/86. First former City stalwart Tommy Booth took over for the remainder of the

1984/85 campaign – one that ended in relegation for the Lilywhites – then former City striker (and ex-Red) Brian Kidd had a go after Booth resigned – but only lasted two months following a dreadful run of results.

ALAN KELLY: KEEPER EXTRAORDINAIRE

Republic of Ireland and North End legend Alan Kelly is one of the best keepers to ever grace Deepdale. He holds the club record for appearances and his sons Alan junior and Gary both went on to become professional keepers. He also played in the 1964 FA Cup final and won the first ever Player of the Year award in 1968. He made 447 league appearances for PNE, but it was his amazing consistency that made him one of the club's best-loved keepers. In five successive seasons from 1966, he missed just five games out of a possible 214 league fixtures and, more impressively, was never dropped.

He is Ireland's third-most capped goalkeeper after Shay Given and Pat Bonner, winning 47 caps for his country and the Town End stand was renamed the Alan Kelly Town End stand in 2001 in his honour. Sadly, Alan passed away in May 2009 – here are a few tributes to the great man:

'He'd just been a great mate since the time I came down to Preston in 1958. We were very close on the field and off the field. He was great, just a nice fella to know.'

Ex-PNE star George Ross

'I will always remember Alan as a charming young man. Many of the lads from Ireland had terrific character and a great sense of humour.'

Former PNE player and manager Tommy Docherty

'He was always ready for a sing-song – he knew the words to every song and he always got us going on the coach on the way back from games. He was a very popular lad and he was well-loved over in Ireland.'

George Ross

'He was one of Ireland's greatest ever goalkeepers. Alan Kelly senior was a former record caps holder and a great servant to Irish football.'

David Blood, former President of the Football Association of Ireland

'As a player, he was one of the best North End have ever had. He wasn't the biggest – but was one of the best.'

Ex-PNE star Frank Lee

'Alan was a fantastic keeper, probably one of the best keepers I ever played with. He was great, a good club lad and used to train hard, was agile and had a lot of natural ability.'

Ex-PNE player John Richards

'Alan Kelly was a great goalkeeper. He rarely made a mistake that led to a goal or us losing a game. He was the absolute epitome of consistency in performance. He set a benchmark which I evaluated my own performances against and in this way, he was a real inspiration.'

Gerry Stewart

PLAYER OF THE YEAR AWARD

Here are the winners of the Preston North End Player of the Year Award since its inception in 1967/68:

1967/68	Alan Kelly
1968/69	Jim McNab
1969/70	Bill Cranston
1970/71	Alan Spavin
1971/72	John McMahon
1972/73	Jim McNab
1973/74	Francis Burns
1974/75	Mike Elwiss
1975/76	Gary Williams
1976/77	Mark Lawrenson
1977/78	Mike Elwiss
1978/79	Mike Robinson
1979/80	Roy Tunks
1980/81	Mick Baxter
1981/82	Don O'Riordan
1982/83	Steve Elliott
1983/84	Peter Litchfield
1984/85	Jonathan Clark
1985/86	John Thomas
1986/87	Gary Brazil
1987/88	Bob Atkins
1988/89	Brian Mooney
1989/90	Warren Joyce
1990/91	Jeff Wrightson
1991/92	Lee Cartwright
1992/93	Tony Ellis
1993/94	Tony Ellis
1994/95	Andy Fensome
1995/96	Andy Saville
1996/97	Sean Gregan
1997/98	Teuvo Moilanen
1998/99	Michael Jackson
1999/2000	Sean Gregan
2000/01	Jonathan Macken
2001/02	Richard Cresswell

2002/03	Chris Lucketti
2003/04	David Healy
2004/05	Youl Mawene
2005/06	Claude Davis
2006/07	Matt Hill
2007/08	Sean St Ledger
2008/09	Jon Parkin
2009/10	Andrew Lonergan

THAT'S ENTERTAINMENT!

In September 2004 Preston North End cheerleaders the Lillies had to disband because seven of the ten members were too busy – working for Perfect 10, a lap-dancing club. Some fans had also written to the club complaining about the cheerleaders sexy antics after one of the members won a 'cleavage of the year' award from a national newspaper. Now North Enders have to make do with Jon Parkin stretches and a rotund steward scratching his backside. The Bill Shankly Kop was sponsored by Perfect 10 in 2006 – one wonders what the great man would have made of that? He'd certainly have come out with a pearl of wisdom of some sort, that's for sure.

SING WHEN YOU'RE WINNING

Two North End players in recent times who have been able to write the theme tune, sing the theme tune – and do the dance – are David Gray and Michael Jackson, though it's not true that the latter where's glittery gloves when the weather becomes inclement.

NICKNAMES

Here are a few nicknames North Enders have given their heroes over the years:

The Preston Plumber – Tom Finney
The Beast – Jon Parkin
Master of the Plastic Pitch – Brian Mooney
Chappy – Les Chapman
The Yorkshire Express – Chris Sedgwick
Cressy/Super Sub – Richard Cresswell

HAPPY CHAPPY!

Les Chapman completed a unique record when he turned out for Preston away to Swansea City on 30 August 1986. A visit to the Vetch Field meant that Chappy had played on all 92 league grounds at that moment in time – an incredible statistic. Even better, North End won 2–1. Chappy retired not long after, a happy man . . .

GENERAL ELECTION

North End took some severe drubbings during the disastrous 1985/86 campaign with the end result seeing the club having to apply for re-election after finishing second bottom of Division Four. Today, that would mean non-league, but at the time, clubs had to seek the support of other clubs in order to maintain their league status. The reason the Lilywhites were in such a dire position was easy to see when you glance at the results that season – here are a selection of the worst (close your eyes and skip to the next page if you're squeamish):

Northampton Town	6–0	PNE
Chester City	6–3	PNE
Walsall	7–3	PNE
Swindon Town	4–1	PNE
Colchester United	4–0	PNE
Aldershot	4–0	PNE

Fortunately, re-election was secured and things slowly improved, but it was, without doubt, the lowest the Lilywhites have ever sunk – and it could have been the end of the club.

THE NATIONAL FOOTBALL MUSEUM

The National Football Museum was built in Preston due to Deepdale being the oldest ground in the world to have been continuously used. A new building was constructed in order to house some of England's most valuable footballing treasures. The permanent collections at the site include artefacts from a wide variety of subject matter, ranging from Wembley to Stanley Matthews. At the same time, the museum hosts many different short-term exhibitions, with many items being borrowed from foreign football associations.

Many different research projects have run in coordination with the museum; some of these studies have resulted in books being published by recognised academics from the University of Central Lancashire.

The offer of free entry was a positive one as it brought almost 120,000 visitors to the museum in its first year in existence. FIFA President Sepp Blatter heaped praise on the venture upon his visit by saying, 'The National Football Museum merits my admiration as a footballer and as the President of FIFA — it is a superb realisation, a real jewel!'

In 2010 the site was closed as Preston and Manchester city Councils discussed the idea of moving the museum to the new Urbis building in Manchester, but confirmation of funding is still to be given. Furthermore, the FA are keen to create a similar museum at the new Wembley in London, which would throw further doubt on the sustainability of the current one in the north.

ALEX BRUCE: PNE LEGEND

Position: Striker
Career: Two spells at PNE (1971–74 and 1975–1983)
Apps: 363
Goals: 157

Born in Dundee in 1952, Alex Bruce spent the whole of his professional career playing football in the north of England and had two spells with Preston North End. An out-and-out striker, Bruce's slight frame did little to hamper his abilities and his eye for goal was more than enough for him to claim a place in the Lancashire club's history. Despite not being the fastest of players, Bruce compensated for this with a vast array of technical ability and acted as an ever-present goal threat whenever he played. Having first appeared for the Lilywhites in 1971, Bruce's goals impressed the Deepdale crowd, before his move to Newcastle United in 1973. His form dipped at St James' Park and the Scot could only manage three goals in twenty appearances.

Bruce's return to Preston seemed to bring about a revival of the striker's goal-scoring instincts. The centre forward's second spell at the club saw him become a fans' favourite and in 2005, when fans voted in a BBC poll to choose the club's cult hero, Bruce came in third position. A goal tally of 135 goals in 301 matches also saw Bruce reach third in a list of Preston's all-time top goalscorers and his partnership with fellow striker Mike Elwiss helped Preston earn promotion to Division Two in 1978. Though Bruce would suffer relegation with the Lilywhites in the 1980/81 season, he is fondly remembered by Preston supporters as the striker who topped the club's goal-scoring chart in seven of his seasons at Deepdale.

Twelve years after first joining the club, Bruce left Preston for a second time in 1983. He was now in his thirties and following a two-year spell at Wigan Athletic, he finished his career with non-league side Rushden and Diamonds.

HANCOCK'S HALF-HOUR

There was nothing humorous about the episode that saw Tony Hancock, a £50,000 buy from Burnley, break his leg in a training ground accident during the 1989/90 season. Hancock clashed with keeper Mark Simpson and spent the next few months with his leg in a plaster cast – a script the lad from East Cheam would have been proud of himself!

EVER-PRESENTS

There have been numerous players in North End's history who have completed an entire league progamme, though none more than Jimmy Trainer who completed seven seasons without missing a game – six of them in succession! Here is the full list including season played and the number of league games played during that particular campaign:

Season	Games	Player(s)
1888/89	22	Jonny Graham & Bob Holmes
1889/90	22	Jack Gordon & Jimmy Trainer
1890/91	22	Bob Holmes & Jimmy Trainer
1891/92	26	Hugh Gallagher, Jimmy Ross, Moses Sanders & Jimmy Trainer
1892/93	30	Jimmy Trainer
1893/94	30	William Greer & Jimmy Trainer
1894/95	30	Jimmy Trainer
1895/96	30	Bob Blyth & Bob Holmes
1896/97	30	Bob Blyth, Jimmy Trainer
1898/99	34	Peter McBride
1899/1900	34	Hugh Dunn & Peter McBride

Season	Games	Player(s)
1902/03	34	Peter McBride, George Tod & Harry Wilcox
1903/04	34	Joseph Derbyshire
1904/05	34	Peter McBride
1911/12	38	William Kirby
1912/13	38	Edward Holdsworth & Charlie McFadyen
1920/21	42	Archie Rawlings
1921/22	42	Tommy Roberts
1922/23	42	Jimmy Branston
1923/24	42	Bobby Crawford & Tommy Roberts
1926/27	42	Bobby Crawford
1927/28	42	Tommy Hamilton & David Morris
1928/29	42	Bobby Crawford
1929/30	42	Bobby Crawford
1930/31	42	Bobby Crawford
1931/32	42	Bobby Crawford

Season	Games	Player(s)
1932/33	42	Frank Gallimore
1933/34	42	Harry Holdcroft & Harry Lowe
1934/35	42	Harry Holdcroft, Harry Lowe & Bill Shankly
1935/36	42	Frank Gallimore, Harry Holdcroft, Harry Lowe & Billy Tremelling
1938/39	42	Frank Gallimore, Harry Holdcroft, Bobby Beattie & George Mutch
1946/47	42	Bill Scott
1950/51	42	Tommy Docherty, Willie Forbes & Angus Morrison
1951/52	42	Willie Cunningham, Tommy Docherty, Joe Marston & Angus Morrison
1952/53	42	Joe Marston, Angus Morrison & Charlie Wayman
1953/54	42	Jimmy Baxter, Joe Marston
1955/56	42	Tommy Thompson
1956/57	42	Fred Else, Joe Walton
1957/58	42	Willie Cunningham, Joe Walton

Season	Games	Player(s)
1958/59	42	Willie Cunningham
1959/60	42	Fred Else, Joe Walton
1961/62	42	Peter Thompson
1962/63	42	Peter Thompson
1963/64	42	George Ross, Tony Singleton
1964/65	42	Alan Spavin
1965/66	42	George Ross
1966/67	42	Ernie Hannigan
1968/69	42	Ken Knighton
1970/71	46	Alan Kelly & Graham Hawkins
1971/72	42	John Bird
1973/74	42	Francis Burns & John McMahon
1974/75	46	John Bird
1975/76	46	Mike Elwiss
1976/77	46	Alex Bruce & Mark Lawrenson
1977/78	46	Mike Elwiss & Roy Tunks
1978/79	42	Roy Tunks

Season	Games	Player(s)
1979/80	42	Steve Elliott & Roy Tunks
1980/81	42	Mick Baxter
1981/82	46	Alex Bruce & Don O'Riorden
1986/87	46	Alex Jones
1989/90	46	Gary Swann
1994/95	42	Andy Fensome
1999/2000	46	Graham Alexander & Michael Jackson
2004/05	46	Youl Mawene
2005/06	39+7	Chris Sedgwick
2008/09	46	Andrew Lonergan & Sean St Ledger

FAITH HEALY

Much-travelled striker David Healy enjoyed his best period at Deepdale and has rarely hit the heights at club level he managed during his time with North End. He was a Lilywhite between 2001 and 2004 and played 138 times, scoring 44 goals and also picked up the 2003/04 PNE Player of the Year award. Healy may have struggled at club level for a number of teams, but he is Northern Ireland's record goalscorer with 35 goals in 80 appearances to date.

THE FOOTBALL WRITERS' ASSOCIATION FOOTBALLER OF THE YEAR

One of the most prestigious awards a professional player can win in England, the Football Writers' Association Footballer of the Year was first awarded in 1947/48 and only eight players have won the honour twice – one being Tom Finney, who became the first person to do so. He first won in 1953/54 and the second occasion was 1957/58. It is perhaps folly to point out he is the only Preston player to ever win the accolade, but there you go!

NOBBLED!

Manager Nobby Stiles came up with the bright idea of every goal scored being sponsored by somebody. He believed it was a novel way to raise funds at a time the club needed them most, but what he hadn't counted on was the ensuing goal drought! North End scored just two goals in eight matches (including four 0–0 draws) after the sponsorship idea was introduced and, thinking it had somehow jinxed the team, the idea was shelved indefinitely!

JUST NOT FINNEY

When North End played away to Cambridge United on 7 October 1978, the hosts scored the only goal of the game to win 1–0. In one of the strange oddities that football sometimes throws up, the winner was scored by Tom Finney – just not *the* Tom Finney, though the odds of this happening must have been pretty long.

QUOTE/UNQUOTE: BILL SHANKLY

'Aye, he's as good as Tommy – but then Tommy's nearly 60 now.'

Shanks when asked about how a football star of the day compared to Tom Finney

'Tom Finney would have been great in any team, in any match and in any age . . . even if he had been wearing an overcoat.'

'I was standing next to Alf Young afterwards. Tears were running down his cheeks. I said to him, "Aye, and that's no' the first one you've given away!"'

On Alf Young's foul which awarded PNE the penalty which won them the FA Cup in 1938

'The sweat poured off us, even though we had short-sleeved jerseys, having learned from the year before. I've still got that silk jersey, made in Preston.'

Reminiscing about the 1938 FA Cup final

'I played it hard, but fair. No cheating.'

'I'd have broken somebody's leg maybe, with a hard tackle, with a bit of spirit, but that's a different story from cheating.'

'You're in, you're out, you've won it and you've hurt him and left him lying there, but it's not a foul because you have timed everything right.'

'As a player I specialised in tackling, which is an art.'

'Congratulations. You are now the greatest right-half in the world. Just put the number 4 shirt on and let it run round, it knows where to go.'

Shanks to Tommy Docherty before he left for Carlisle

'Tom Finney would go through a mountain.'

On Tom Finney's courage on the field

QUOTE/UNQUOTE: TOM FINNEY

'It was only 15 or 16 matches but even so it's a fantastic achievement and it's important we remember that and that the youngsters read about it.'

On 'The Invincibles' winning the double

'He would tell us that he felt proud watching us and that we played for a great club. It lifted you six feet because as a junior you looked up to those sorts of people.'

On Bill Shankly's interaction with the youth players despite being a 'big name' at the club

'It was the management that had all the power in those days and now of course it's turned complete circle and it's the players who have the power.'

'I was going past a defender and the ball ran into a pool of water. It was a fantastic photograph and it won the Sports Photograph of the Year award. The sculpture is a true likeness.'

On 'The Splash' sculpture which now sits outside the National Football Museum at Deepdale

QUOTE/UNQUOTE: PETER THOMPSON

'At Preston, most of the team was getting old and I was told my chance would come fairly soon, and I think that signing for PNE was one of the best things I ever did.'

'I was part of the fabulous side that reached the final of the FA Youth Cup, and I've got some great memories . . . including the return leg of the final against Chelsea where there were something like 25,000 people inside Deepdale.'

'I was dead happy at North End except for a lot of the football, which is an important consideration!'

'I always felt I was a useless defender!'
On being played in defence at PNE despite thinking he was a more attacking player

QUOTE/UNQUOTE: JOE MARSTON

'It turned out that my friend had got in touch with Blackpool who said "thanks but no thanks", but reckoned that Preston would probably be interested. One club didn't want me but the other one did, and that's how it all started.'

'We were met at the station by two directors, and there were quite a lot of other people there waiting to witness our arrival – probably about 150 or so – and I think they probably thought I was a kangaroo that was going to come bouncing off the train!'
On his arrival at PNE from Australia

'So when half time came round they just put whisky on the cut as a disinfectant and then gave me a swig before they put the stitches in. Then I went back out for the second half!'

On injuring his leg during a match

'Captaining Preston was a brilliant honour because the Preston people really took to me and made my family feel really welcome.

'I also follow the team's results very keenly in the papers, but that's been pretty awful at times this season – I think the side needs a Charlie Wayman!'

'I still speak very highly of Preston because it was the chance of a lifetime – and it came good.'

'One of the other things that stands out is my last game at Deepdale when I'd announced I was going home at the end of the season. I can still picture standing there in the middle of the field as the crowd sang "Waltzing Matilda" and "For He's A Jolly Good Fellow".'

'There were some big moments in my career like playing in the World Cup with Australia, but the proudest moments were at Preston.'

QUOTE/UNQUOTE: MIKE CONROY

'There was one training session he conducted where he made us all play one touch, and every touch a striker made had to go forward – you can work that one out!'

On then manager John Beck's training methods

'It's an honour and a privilege to have played for Preston North End. When you scored a goal, you knew that the people celebrating around you were loving watching the goal as much as you'd enjoyed scoring it.'

'It's funny but my wife was looking around on Google the other night and she came across the goal on the internet. My daughter wasn't born until that December, and she found it pretty hard to believe that there I was scoring that goal in front of her on the screen!'

On his 1994 FA Cup goal v Blackpool

'They and Burnley are two huge clubs with great histories, and the thing I loved about playing for both clubs is that the people who support them are absolutely fantastic.'

QUOTE/UNQUOTE: MICHAEL JACKSON

'I had some great times there that will never be forgotten, I love the place.'

'Most Preston fans probably think they should be in the top four or five all season but if you look at the resources and cash that's spent in that league it's not always possible, especially if you look at the players that they've lost since they were last in the play-offs.'

'One of the highlights of my time there was the whole experience of watching the club grow from when I [was] first there with one stand developed to when I left when most of it had been done. They are moving forward but it can only be done slowly.'

DAVID HEALY: PNE LEGEND

Position: Striker
Career at PNE: 2000–4
Apps: 138
Goals: 44

A player who has always shone brightest on the international stage, David Healy's most impressive spell of domestic form came during his time at Deepdale. The Northern Irish international became Preston's record signing in 2001 when he joined from Manchester United for a fee of £1.5m, only days after initially moving on loan (in late 2000). This was the first time Preston had ever spent more than a million pounds on a player – their previous record fee being only a third of that when they signed Michael Appleton for £500,000 in 1997. The striker soon found his feet for the Lilywhites and during his three-and-a-half years at the club, Healy scored 44 goals. Healy's goalscoring exploits helped North End reach the 2001 play-off final, only to be beaten 3–0 by Bolton Wanderers.

Following an inconsistent spell for the club, Healy was loaned out to Norwich City in 2003 and eventually left for Leeds United a year later. The Northern Irishman returned to form at Elland Road but again couldn't help his side progress past the play-off final. In 2007, Leeds were relegated from the Championship and Healy left for Premier League side Fulham, having finished the season as Leeds' top scorer. The striker never truly settled into Premier League life, neither at Fulham, nor during a spell with Sunderland and returned to the Championship in 2010 when he joined Ipswich Town on loan.

Despite inconsistencies at domestic level, Northern Ireland's all-time top goalscorer also holds the record for most goals in a European Championship qualifying campaign. Healy's 13 goals surpassed the previous record of 12, held by Croatia's Davor Suker. 'Sir David' as he is referred to by Northern Irish football fans received an MBE in 2008 for services to football and the community in Northern Ireland.

THE ANGLO-SCOTTISH CUP

North End took part in three Anglo-Scottish Cup tournaments without ever troubling the trophy engravers. In 1978/79 the Lilywhites at least had the pleasure of beating Blackpool 4–2 before losing to Burnley and Blackburn and spinning out of the competition. A year later, Preston again beat Blackpool, this time 3–1, then drew 1–1 at Blackburn before beating Burnley 2–1 at Turf Moor to progress to the quarter-finals. Unfortunately, mighty Morton won both legs – 3–1 at Deepdale and 2–1 in the return – to progress 5–2 on aggregate.

North End's last attempt to win the cup was in 1980/81, but a 0–0 draw with Carlisle was the only positive of the group stages, with both Blackpool and Blackburn winning 1–0 at Deepdale.

The total Anglo-Scottish Cup record is:

P: 10   W: 3   D: 2   L: 5   F: 14   A: 15

QUOTE/UNQUOTE: WARREN JOYCE

'I thought John McGrath was the best manager I played for. I thought he was very good. It was a very enjoyable time for me, with the combination of him and Les Chapman.'

'Everyone in that team had the standard, I mean the training was ferocious, if you did anything wrong or there was anything messed up people were on your back but in a good way.'

On the 2000/01 side

'The last season I was there, I had a horrific injury and it was either I get off the plastic or I was finished, and I think that happened to one or two of the lads at the time. It probably destroyed Brian Mooney's knees and it had a massive detrimental affect on my back. That was the only reason I left the football club really.'

'It is a bit weird coming back to the stadium and seeing it. It almost doesn't feel like you've played there because everything is so vastly improved and new. You kind of miss seeing the old stand opposite, but things progress and get better.'

'It was a club I really enjoyed being at and I have a lot of affinity with and I am delighted to see them doing so well right now.'

FA YOUTH CUP

North End's only appearance in the FA Youth Cup final was in 1950 when Chelsea triumphed in a two-legged final. The Lilywhites beat Liverpool and Manchester United along the way and things looked good after the first leg at Stamford Bridge ended in a 1–1 draw. But it was Chelsea who ran out 4–1 winners in the return game at Deepdale in front of a 27,000 crowd to take the trophy 5–2 on aggregate.

FA CHARITY SHIELD

The Lilywhites' only Charity Shield appearance was in 1938 when Ted Drake's double gave Arsenal a 2–1 win – Bobby Beattie having replied for North End. The team was: Holdcroft, Gallimore, A. Beattie, Shankly, Batey, Milne, McGibbons, Mutch, Dougal, R. Beattie, Maxwell.

OH WE DON'T LIKE TO BE BESIDE THE SEASIDE!

Preston's fiercest rivals are without doubt Blackpool FC. Over the years the two clubs have met in each of England's four divisions. The Lilywhites have an extremely good record against the Seasiders, which makes it harder for PNE fans to accept the recent good fortunes of their neighbours. Many locals call it the 'M55 Derby' due to the motorway running between the cities.

Matches between the clubs have unfortunately led to violent clashes taking place between the two sets of fans. The most famous – and painful – game between the clubs was in 1970 when Blackpool won 3–0 to clinch promotion, which at the same time relegated PNE. Over 30 players have represented both clubs; most recently Brett Ormerod left the Lilywhites for the Seasiders in 2009.

Tom Finney described the rivalry thus, 'We always saw Blackpool as our main rivals and we had some great matches against them. But there was none of the current nastiness from some fans.'

The most extreme example of the rivalry was Preston boss Gary Peter's vow to not mention Blackpool's name in public, instead describing them as 'That lot down the M55.'

PNE's all-time record against Blackpool is:
P: 93   W: 44   D: 18   L: 31

The fact that Lancashire is a veritable hotbed of football means that the clubs share a rivalry with a collection of other clubs especially Blackburn and Burnley, but the rivalry with these sides come nowhere near that of the rocky relationship with the Tangerines.

TOTAL LEAGUE RECORD TO END OF 2009/10 CAMPAIGN

If anyone ever needed to be reminded of Preston's proud past, perhaps at a glance at the all-time league table will remind one or two people just how successful the Lilywhites have been over the years. North End stand at the 5th best team _ever_ in England, behind only Manchester United, Liverpool, Arsenal and Wolverhampton Wanderers.

The overall record is:
Played: 4,550
Home: W: 1,221 D: 568 L: 486 F: 4,235 A: 2,540
Away: W: 553 D: 573 L: 1,149 F: 2,568 A: 3,883
Total Pts: 5,205
GD: +380

In the FA Cup, Preston North End are 16th having won 159 of their 334 ties, drawing 62 and losing 113. The goals scored are 646 and 441 conceded. In the League Cup North End are the 45th most successful side having won 57 of their 146 ties, drawing 33 and losing 56. There have been 198 goals scored and 226 conceded so far.

The overall record, then, of Preston's existence as a professional club, in all league and domestic competitions up to the end of the 2009/10 season, is:

P: 5,030   W: 1,990   D: 1,236   L: 1,804
F: 7,647   A: 6,423

GET YOUR KIT ON!

Former North End player and manager Les Chapman has been Manchester City's kit manager since 1997. 'Chappy' is one of City's biggest and most popular characters and was given a Lifetime Achievement Award in 2010 for his service to the Blues. Though his time at Deepdale only lasted a couple of seasons, he still made 53 appearances during that time, scoring once. Chappy then became boss from 1990 to 1992 before being sacked in October 1992.

QUOTE/UNQUOTE: TEUVO (TEPI) MOILANEN

'Preston were a very ambitious club and it was an easy step to make, it was a big step forward but it was a step into the unknown so to speak.'

'I played easily the best matches of my career there and it is definitely the footballing home for me in terms of my career.'

'I came there with little football education and that's where I learned the game.'

'Preston were a successful club during that season and it was easy to come to a winning club at that time which was well-organised.'

'PNE were going through a successful period so it made it even more special for myself in a club that was winning all the time and going forward.'

'I still think that the celebrations and the atmosphere at the party for the Third Division win was possibly the highlight of my stay; it was the first real success that Preston had had in years and I rate it higher than the second division promotion.'

'There's no point going over the ifs and buts – if we had been luckier with the other teams we may have had a better chance but at the end of the day you have to build success in a way that will last and perform it over a longer period of time.'

On missing out on promotion to the Premier League

QUOTE/UNQUOTE

'It's been an honour to work there; it's been a privilege to work there. I know we've worked as hard as we possibly could, myself and the staff, to turn things around.'

'It's been a good experience and I've learnt a hell of a lot – good and bad.'

Paul Simpson

'The club is very ambitious, with a very ambitious manager.'

Paul Hayes

'This is a great club with a great stadium, great fans and a good bunch of players.'

Neill Collins

'I had the opportunity to leave, I chose to stay and I have not regretted that for a moment and I am not looking to move.'

'It's nice people feel I'm doing a good enough job to link me with other jobs but until I hear anything different I am happy doing my job here.'

'I've got a fantastic job and I wouldn't have come to the decision I've come to if I didn't think that I could move the club on.'

'This is a fantastic challenge and if I thought there was no chance of progressing the club further then that might have pushed me to move.'

'I see a bright future at Preston. I'm hoping that we can get to the Premiership – it's the reason I took the job.'

'We obviously all want to make as much progress as we possibly can, as quickly as we can.'

Alan Irvine

'With a free transfer at the end of the season you become appealing to a lot of clubs but for me it was always about staying here and wanting to get this done as soon as possible.'

Andy Lonergan

'I'm pleased to have reached the 100-game mark and hopefully there will be plenty more games to come.'

'I'm happy at Preston and I've been featuring in a lot of games which is something I obviously enjoy.'
Neil Mellor – just before he went out in loan to Sheffield Wednesday due to lack of opportunities at Deepdale!

'I am really chuffed that I have signed a contract, got a new deal and hopefully now I will try and keep playing well, take us up the table and try and get promotion.'
Sean St Ledger

'The reason I am coming down to Preston is because they are a good team, they are ambitious and they want to do things.'
Wayne Brown

'It seems that every year Preston are doing well and fighting for a top-six finish.'
Jay McEveley

'Obviously I'm delighted with the move. I spoke to the manager and he sold the club to me.'

'I had the chance to go to a club down south, but Preston appealed to me much more.'

'Everything is geared up for a Premier League football club here.
Jon Parkin

'I think there is a confidence in the team that we can go to places and claim victory.'
Chris Brown

'It's quite an exciting time to be here at the minute.'

'It would obviously be nice for me to play out the latter days of my career playing for Preston in the Premier League. That would be the icing on the cake for me, and I think the club's now going the right way to achieve that.'

Paul McKenna

'The one thing since I have been at Preston is that if you do well they will look after you.'

'When you have 10 or 12 months left on your contract they come and see you and try and sort something out and it gives you that security, it also makes you feel wanted and that's a big part of being here.'

Callum Davidson

THE INVINCIBLES

One of only two sides ever to have achieved the feat in English top flight history, the 1888/89 Preston North End side earned the title of 'The Invincibles' having won the league without losing a single game. Under the guidance of Major William Sudell, the Lancashire club improved vastly during their early years and the signings of George Drummond, John Gordon and David Russell soon made Preston a giant of amateur football. Sudell's ability to persuade top Scottish players to cross the border and join Deepdale aided the Lilywhites in their domination of the amateur game, though Sudell's approach was widely criticised by rival clubs.

In 1883, the press first coined the 'Invincibles' nickname as a sneer against Preston for paying footballers to play for their club. Many at the time felt that this 'professionalism' was a way of gaining an advantage that other clubs simply couldn't afford and this bad feeling towards Sudell and his team culminated in January 1884 when, having been beaten by Preston in the FA Cup, West Ham United reported their opponents to the FA for having fielded a professional side.

It took another three years for the Football League to be established and in 1888, Preston were named a founder member of the professional game. The league consisted of twelve clubs and offered the club a much-needed challenge having won forty-two consecutive games the previous season. It turned out that Preston's good form would continue and in 1889 the Lilywhites were named the first ever Football League Champions, having gone the whole season unbeaten. Jimmy Ross, John Goodall and Fred Dewhurst all starred for the club that year, scoring fifty-three goals between them and leading their side to eighteen wins in twenty-two league matches. Not only was Sudell's side never beaten, but they also won 7–0 on two separate occasions to enhance their superiority over their fellow league members.

The club's outstanding league form was mirrored, if not bettered, by their FA Cup run which concluded in March 1889 with a 3–0 win over Wolverhampton Wanderers. A run of five wins without conceding a goal led them to FA Cup glory and to them being named the first ever English club to achieve the 'double'. The 'Invincible' side of 1888/89 has forever been remembered by the Preston North End faithful and in 2008, Deepdale's latest stand was named the The Invincibles Pavilion, in honour of the club's most famous side.

Club legends such as Finney, Shankly and Kelly would eventually bring success of another kind to the

Lancashire club, though none would ever match the success of Sudell's team. In fact, it would be another 105 years before any other top-flight English side would repeat the feat and even Arsenal's 2003/04 squad couldn't match Preston's 'double' success during their unbeaten campaign.

WHEN BECKS WAS A LILYWHITE ...

Having shone as a member of the 1992 FA Youth Cup-winning side, a young David Beckham showed early potential which would one day see him win a Champions League medal and captain his country. In early 1995, Manchester United manager Sir Alex Ferguson decided that the best way for Beckham to develop was to seek first-team football elsewhere. The United starlet had already proved himself capable of competing with the very best, having scored against Galatasaray on his Champions League debut in December 1994, and Preston North End were not willing to miss out on the opportunity to nurture such a promising talent.

The future England skipper laid down a marker on his league debut for the Lilywhites, scoring directly from a corner kick. Combined with skill, pace and an eye for a pass, Beckham instantly found himself in favour with the Preston faithful and continued to impress during the rest of his time at the club. The world's most famous footballer only played five times for North End but scored again in his second game and assisted four more goals in total.

Beckham's time at Deepdale was cut short after Alex Ferguson found himself without a number of first-team players and as a result, chose to recall the midfielder. The experience at Preston was evidently of great benefit to the free-kick specialist as he was handed his Premier League debut upon his return to Old Trafford in April 1995. Alongside Nicky Butt and the Neville brothers, Beckham progressed from United's academy to become a member of one of the most successful English sides in recent history, though the story could have been very different had Preston offered the £3m that United are rumored to have been willing to accept for the future Real Madrid and AC Milan favourite.

QUOTE/UNQUOTE: MARK LAWRENSON

'Bobby Charlton signed me and there's actually a quiz question out there asking "Which footballer played for both Bobby and Jack Charlton?"'

'When I actually made my [Ireland] debut, I'd played for Preston on the Saturday, flew to Dublin on the Saturday night, played against Poland on the Sunday, flew back home on Monday and played for Preston again on the Tuesday evening.'

On being recommended for Ireland by then PNE manager Alan Kelly

SIR TOM FINNEY: PNE LEGEND

Nationality: English
Date of Birth: 5 April 1922
Position: Striker
Career at PNE: 1946–60
Appearances: 433
Goals: 187

The most famous player ever to have plied his trade at
Deepdale is club all-time top goalscorer Sir Tom Finney.
The Englishman, who was born and raised around the
corner from the club's Deepdale ground, spent 14 years
with Preston and is considered to be the greatest player
ever to line up for the Lancashire club. The 'Preston
Plumber', who was knighted for his services to sport in
1998, originally joined the club in 1939 but had to wait
seven years before making his league debut. This was due
to the outbreak of the Second World War, which caused
league football to be suspended. One month later, having
made a name for himself in wartime tournaments,
Finney made his England debut and went on to make 76
appearances at national level, scoring 30 goals.

During his time at the club, Preston won only the War
League Cup and a Second Division Championship, yet
despite this relative lack of success, Finney was fiercely
loyal to his boyhood club. This was proved in 1952
when Italian side Palermo made a bid for the forward.
Despite the opportunity to play on a 'bigger stage', he
chose to remain at Deepdale and was duly rewarded in
1954 when he won the Footballer of the Year award.
This came as consolation to Finney who had lost 3–2 to
West Brom in the FA Cup final that same season. In 1957,
three years before retiring with a persistent groin injury,
Finney became the first player to be named Footballer of

the Year for a second time. The current club president did come out of retirement in 1963 to play a one-off European clash for Irish side Distillery, but is forever considered to be the model 'one-club' man by Preston North End fans.

QUOTE/UNQUOTE: BJARKI GUNNLAUGSSON

'I knew it was one of the oldest clubs in the world, a traditional club. I knew about Tom Finney and the good players who had played for them.'

'I had a short time there but it was a really fantastic period and I hope they get promotion as soon as possible.'

'I turned down a move to Kilmarnock to join Preston and at the time some people questioned that because PNE were in the second division and Kilmarnock were in the Scottish Premier League, but there was something about the club, you knew it was going to be a success story.'

'As soon as I arrived I could see the potential for the club and it was a lovely stadium with perfect grass at the ground, a great manager and you knew that something was happening there.'

record for most league appearances (447) and is fondly remembered by football fans of many clubs, not just Preston North End.

Despite success early in his career with Drumcondra, Kelly only ever won a Third Division championship medal during his fifteen years at Deepdale and is better remembered for being a losing finalist in the club's 1964 FA Cup final appearance against West Ham. On a more personal note, however, Kelly was named the club's first ever Player of the Year in 1968, five years before a shoulder injury ended his career in 1973.

Kelly remained at the club, however, as a part of their coaching staff and was later promoted to assistant manager by Nobby Stiles in 1977. One year before taking over as caretaker manager of Preston in 1981, Kelly had a one-match spell in the same post with his national side. In 1983, Kelly was named the permanent manager of Preston but lasted only two years. His short time as manager did nothing to hinder his popularity at Deepdale and in 2001, the Deepdale Alan Kelly Town End was unveiled.

The Preston favourite spent the final years of his life living in the USA before he sadly passed away in May 2009.

QUOTE/UNQUOTE: KURT NOGAN

'The North End fans were some of the best supporters I ever played in front of.'

'I'm glad I made the move because when I signed I was a bit dubious, but it was one of the best moves I made and when Moyesie took over it was great.'

'When I was at Preston our attitude was to win our home games and to make sure we didn't lose our away games, so if we went away and got two draws on the bounce and won at home you could see the difference in the table.'

'I will never forget my times at Preston; hopefully they'll be in the Premiership soon.'

LES DAGGER: PNE LEGEND

Nationality: English
Position: Right winger
Career at PNE: 1956–60
Appearances: 72
Goals: 10
Joined: From West Auckland FC for £50
Left: To Carlisle United for £750

As an amateur, Dagger plied his trade with Bolton Wanderers' 'A' team before national service saw him move to Barnard Castle. Dagger was later signed by West Auckland football club and, while playing in a cup final against rivals Bishop Auckland, caught the eye of both Sunderland and Preston. Despite a move to the north-east seemingly on the cards, Preston negotiated well and persuaded Dagger to move to Deepdale instead. The Lilywhites paid an initial £50 which eventually rose to £200.

As fate would have it, Dagger made his debut for Preston against Sunderland in November 1956, after team-mate Les Campbell was called away to complete his national service. Dagger's ability to assist goals soon established him as Preston's first-choice right winger, though it is important to note that in 72 appearances for the club, he scored 10 goals himself. Dagger only just missed out on the league title in both his first seasons at Preston, finishing third and second respectively.

In 1960, following relegation, Dagger was one of a number of players off-loaded by the club and he found himself transferred to Carlisle United for a fee of only £750. The sale of Dagger was bemoaned by many North End fans at the time and after their former player helped Carlisle win promotion in his first season at the club, the Deepdale faithful seemed to be proved right in considering this a piece of bad business.

GET YOUR SKATES OFF – NOW!

In an unusual step that seems almost too obvious to enforce, all North End players were banned from using roller-skates in 1929. Hard to imagine a player would attempt to have a sly roll here and there, but the popularity of the sport at the time, coupled with a spate of reported injuries arising from skating, resulted in a ban. If a player even looks at a pair of rollerblades today he is fined a week's wages – and that's a Rafa Benitez fact!

GEORGE ROSS: PNE LEGEND

Nationality: Scottish
Date of Birth: 15 April 1943
Position: Full-back
Career at PNE: 1960–73
Appearances: 441
Goals: 3
Left: To Southport in 1973

Ross was a product of the successful Preston North End academy which competed in the FA Youth Cup final in 1960. Following an impressive run of displays for the youth team, the full-back was introduced to the senior side and was included on the tour to Switzerland in the summer of 1960. Ross impressed while playing alongside the senior squad players but with club favourite Willie Cunningham occupying the number two shirt, it wasn't until May 1963 that Ross fully established himself.

As a member of that 1964 FA Cup final squad, Ross suffered the heartbreak of falling at the final hurdle, while also being relegated twice as a Lilywhite. He also experienced the joy of winning the Third Division Championship however, and as a result, gaining promotion in 1970/71. After thirteen years, the Scottish full-back was released by Preston and made the move to Southport. Here he spent three seasons before finally moving to Morecambe.

Ross' service has never been forgotten and – as of 2010 – he still worked for the club on match days. In January 1998 he was named the Chairman of the Preston North End Former Players' Association and in April 2009, received the Preston North End Lifetime Achievement Award.

TOMMY THOMPSON: PNE LEGEND

Nationality: English
Date of Birth: 10 November 1928
Position: Inside Forward
Career at PNE: 1955–61
Appearances: 188
Goals: 117
Joined: From Aston Villa for £27,000 in May 1955
Left: For Stoke City in 1961

Tommy Thompson spent six years at Deepdale when he eventually signed from Aston Villa in 1955, but he would have joined much earlier had he had his way. In 1950, Thompson was a Newcastle United player on the verge of leaving St James' Park. At that time, both Villa and Preston had expressed an interest. It is rumored that Thompson had made his mind up to join Preston before North End then reneged on their interest claiming 'the timing was not right.'

The inside forward finally made the move to Deepdale however, for a fee of £27,000. On debut against Everton, it took him only two minutes to score his first goal for his new club. Thompson went on to score 23 more goals that year and finished the 1957/58 campaign as leading scorer. Thompson and club legend Tom Finney once combined to score 60 altogether (Thompson scoring 34 of them).

'Topper', as he was affectionately known by the Preston faithful, was a constant threat to opposing teams and holds the club record for goals in consecutive games (11). He left the club having scored 117 goals in 188 league games for Preston. In 1961, the England international moved to Stoke and then on to Barrow in 1963, but a knee injury brought an end to his career.

MARK LAWRENSON: PNE LEGEND

Nationality: Irish (though born in England)
Date of Birth: 2 June 1957
Position: Defender
Career at PNE: 1974–7
Appearances: 73
Goals: 2
Left: To Brighton & Hove Albion for £100,000

Mark Lawrenson may have only spent three years as a player at Deepdale, but in this short space of time, the Lilywhite supporter made his mark and has never stopped championing his side since leaving.

Son of Tom Lawrenson, a former North End winger, Mark joined his boyhood club in 1974, while Bobby Charlton was still at the helm. He firmly established himself as a crucial member of the Preston defence and quickly became a fans' favourite.

During his time at Deepdale, goalkeeping coach and Preston legend Alan Kelly recommended him to the Irish national boss having discovered his Irish family relations. Lawrenson debuted for Ireland in April 1977. Lawrenson's excellent season culminated in him being awarded the Preston North End Player of the Year award.

Lawrenson had such a good season that Liverpool came calling. They were to be outbid by Brighton who spent £100,000 on the Irish defender. Four years later however, Brighton found themselves in financial difficulties and were forced to sell their star players. Liverpool again expressed an interest and gained Lawrenson's services for £900,000 – £800,000 more than Brighton had spent four years earlier.

The defender went on to win numerous honours with the most successful Liverpool side ever and remains a popular *Match of the Day* pundit to this day.

WILLIE CUNNINGHAM: PNE LEGEND

Nationality: Scottish
Date of Birth: 22 February 1925
Date of Death: 15 November 2000
Position: Full-back
Career at PNE: 1949–63
Appearances: 487
Goals: 3
Joined: From Airdrie United for £5,000 in June 1949
Left: To Southport

Scottish full-back Willie Cunningham became a firm favourite at Deepdale during his fourteen years at the club having been bought in 1949 for a fee of £5,000. Cunningham spent the first three professional years of his career in his native Scotland playing for both Dunfermline Athletic and Airdrie United, but it wasn't until his move to England that he was recognised by his national squad. Despite having developed as a centre-back, Cunningham soon made the transition to full-back and became one of the most talented defenders in the country.

In 1954, the Scot was part of the Preston squad which lost in the FA Cup final to West Bromwich Albion. That summer, however, Cunningham received some consolation by traveling to the World Cup finals as captain of the Scottish national side. On 18 April 1961, Cunningham made his 400th appearance against Bolton and played at the club for another two years before leaving to become player/manager of Southport in 1963, where he stayed until 1965. On 21 October 1963, Preston played a testimonial against an invitational XI in aid of Cunningham. The Preston favourite later returned to the club as a reserve team trainer.

TANGERINE SCREAM

It was fitting that North End faced a goalkeeper called Wolf for the October 1929 visit of Blackpool because the Deepdale fans were howling with misery all the way home after their first-ever home defeat to the Seasiders.

If there was one minor consolation, it was that the game produced ten goals and was a rollercoaster from start to finish. That the score ended 6–4 to Blackpool when the score was 0–0 with 35 minutes played is incredible, with all ten goals scored in the remaining 55 minutes. The visitors edged ahead with two quick goals but it was nip and tuck all the way and 3–4 at one point before the eventual Second Division champions pulled clear to lead 6–3 though North End scored once more before the final whistle. It was Blackpool's first ever win in the league at Deepdale and thus ended a very happy run for the Lilywhites. Things would never be the same again. . .

QUOTE/UNQUOTE: DARREN FERGUSON

'I feel that having only had one manager's job that to get this one as my second one is a massive privilege and I am very lucky.'

'There are good people here; I have sensed that during my first day of being here.'

'I want to win games and I want them [the fans] to be entertained – I am not saying they haven't been, but that is just the philosophy I am very strong on and hopefully it will be the case.'

'I don't want to see people walking around Preston with Man United shirts on, I want to see them with Preston shirts on and we want to get to that promised land, it has to be the ambition.'

'I think the club is capable of making that next step. It is where I want to work, and we have a good chance.'

'I said in the press conference that this is a club you aspire to. It is a well-established and well-regarded football club. It is a family club and it has a decent fan base and that is how people perceive it from the outside.'

'We have a really, really good team spirit and togetherness and that's important.'

GRAHAM ALEXANDER: PNE LEGEND

Nationality: Scottish (though born in England)
Date of Birth: 10 October 1971
Position: Right-back
Career at PNE: 1999–2007
Appearances: 400
Goals: 52
Joined: From Luton Town
Left: To Burnley for £200,000

Former club captain Graham Alexander joined the club in 1999 from Luton Town, having turned down the opportunity to play for Lancashire rivals Burnley. The Scottish international became a stalwart of the Preston side who spent years attempting to win promotion to the Premier League and his defensive capabilities were very rarely in question at Deepdale. The penalty kick specialist was a member of the squad which won promotion to Division One in 2000 and then played a part in four years of second-tier play-offs during his eight-year tenure.

Alexander never took Preston over the finishing line, though did achieve individual success in 2005 when he was included in the 2004/05 Championship Team of the Season. During his time at Preston, Alexander made a number of appearances for his country. Having debuted in 2002 against Nigeria, the Scottish defender has featured forty more times for his country, notably in Scotland's 1–0 win over France in Scotland's Euro 2008 qualifying group.

In August 2007, Alexander played his 400th and final game for North End as he was sold to Burnley, eight years after they'd first approached him. Before Burnley signed the Scot, Crystal Palace had had a bid for Alexander rejected, Preston claiming that they were not willing to sell their captain. Preston explained the decision to sell Alexander was as a result of difficulties in contract negotiations. Finally in August 2009, Alexander, having helped Burnley earn their place in the Premier League, became the league's oldest debutant ever.

DON'T QUOTE ME ...

'They offered me a handshake of £10,000 to settle amicably. I told them they would have to be a lot more amicable than that.'

Tommy Docherty on being sacked by North End in 1981

'One of this season's discoveries, Bill Shankly, played with rare tenacity and uncommonly good ideas for a lad of twenty. He is full of good football and possessed with unlimited energy; he should go far.'

How right he was! Preston North End's correspondent, Walter Pilkington on the Scot's first campaign at Deepdale

'As a right-winger converted from a left-footer, he was the best centre forward I've ever seen!'

Jimmy McIlroy, Burnley and Northern Ireland international

'Dichio, Dichio, Danny Dichio, he's got no hair, but we don't care, Danny Dichio!'

Preston fans, after the folically challenged striker scored against Sunderland

'Tom Finney should claim income tax relief . . . for his 10 dependants.'

An anonymous observation on the weakness of the Preston team in his absence

If all the brains in the game sat in committee to design the perfect player, they would come up with a reincarnation of Tom Finney.'

Anonymous newspaper feature

'It was usually considered that a winger should be a provider, but I always worked on the theory that the man in the best position should accept the responsibility.'

Tom Finney

INTERNATIONAL FINNEY

Here is a record of each of Tom Finney's England appearances including cap number (C), goals scored (G) and goal tally (T) . . .

C	G	T	Date	Venue	Opponent	Score	Comp
1	1	1	28/9/46	Belfast	N. Ireland	7–2	British Championship
2	1	2	30/9/46	Dublin	Ireland	1–0	
3	-	2	13/11/46	Manchester	Wales	3–0	British Championship
4	1	3	27/11/46	Huddersfield	Netherlands	8–2	
5	1	4	3/5/47	London	France	3–0	
6	1	5	25/5/47	Lisbon	Portugal	10–0	
7	2	7	21/9/47	Brussels	Belgium	5–2	
8	1	8	18/10/47	Cardiff	Wales	3–0	British Championship

C	G	T	Date	Venue	Opponent	Score	Comp
9	-	8	5/11/47	Liverpool	N. Ireland	2–2	British Championship
10	-	8	19/11/47	London	Sweden	4–2	
11	1	9	10/4/48	Glasgow	Scotland	2–0	British Championship
12	2	11	16/5/48	Turin	Italy	4–0	
13	-	11	9/10/48	Belfast	N. Ireland	6–2	British Championship
14	1	12	11/10/48	Birmingham	Wales	1–0	British Championship
15	-	12	9/4/48	London	Scotland	1–3	British Championship
16	1	13	15/5/49	Stockholm	Sweden	1–3	
17	1	14	18/5/49	Oslo	Norway	4–1	
18	-	14	22/5/49	Paris	France	3–1	
19	-	14	21/9/49	Liverpool	Ireland	0–2	
20	-	14	15/10/49	Cardiff	Wales	4–2	World Cup Qualifier
21	-	14	16/11/49	Manchester	N. Ireland	9–2	World Cup Qualifier
22	-	14	30/11/49	London	Italy	2–0	
23	-	14	15/4/50	Glasgow	Scotland	1–0	World Cup Qualifier
24	4	18	14/5/50	Lisbon	Portugal	5–3	
25	-	18	18/5/50	Brussels	Belgium	4–1	
26	-	18	25/6/50	Rio	Chile	2–0	World Cup
27	-	18	26/6/50	Belo Horizonte	USA	0–1	World Cup
28	-	18	2/7/50	Rio	Spain	0–1	World Cup
29	-	18	15/11/50	Sunderland	Wales	4–2	British Championship
30	1	19	14/4/51	London	Scotland	2–3	British Championship
31	-	19	9/5/51	London	Argentina	2–1	
32	1	20	19/5/51	Liverpool	Portugal	5–2	

C	G	T	Date	Venue	Opponent	Score	Comp
33	-	20	3/10/51	London	France	2–2	
34	-	20	20/10/51	Cardiff	Wales	1–1	British Championship
35	-	20	14/11/51	Birmingham	N. Ireland	2–0	British Championship
36	-	20	5/4/52	Glasgow	Scotland	2–1	British Championship
37	-	20	18/5/52	Florence	Italy	1–1	
38	-	20	25/5/52	Vienna	Austria	3–2	
39	-	20	28/5/52	Zürich	Switzerland	3–0	
40	-	20	4/10/52	Belfast	N. Ireland	2–2	British Championship
41	1	21	12/11/52	London	Wales	5–2	British Championship
42	-	21	26/11/52	London	Belgium	5–0	
43	-	21	18/4/53	London	Scotland	2–2	British Championship
44	-	21	17/5/53	Buenos Aires	Argentina	0–0	
45	-	21	24/5/53	Santiago	Chile	2–1	
46	-	21	31/5/53	Montevideo	Uruguay	1–2	
47	2	23	8/6/53	New York	USA	6–3	
48	-	23	10/10/53	Cardiff	Wales	4–1	World Cup Qualifier
49	-	23	3/4/54	Glasgow	Scotland	4–2	World Cup Qualifier
50	-	23	16/5/54	Belgrade	Yugoslavia	0–1	
51	-	23	23/5/54	Budapest	Hungary	1–7	
52	-	23	17/6/54	Basel	Belgium	4–4	World Cup
53	-	23	20/6/54	Bern	Switzerland	2–0	World Cup
54	1	24	26/6/54	Basel	Uruguay	2–4	World Cup
55	-	24	1/12/54	London	W. Germany	3–1	
56	-	24	2/10/55	Copenhagen	Denmark	5–1	
57	-	24	22/10/55	Cardiff	Wales	1–2	British Championship

C	G	T	Date	Venue	Opponent	Score	Comp
58	1	25	2/11/55	London	N. Ireland	3–0	British Championship
59	1	26	30/11/55	London	Spain	4–1	
60	-	26	14/4/56	Glasgow	Scotland	1–1	British Championship
61	1	27	14/11/56	London	Wales	3–1	British Championship
62	-	27	28/11/56	London	Yugoslavia	3–0	
63	-	27	5/12/56	Wolv'n	Denmark	5–2	World Cup Qualifier
64	-	27	6/4/57	London	Scotland	2–1	British Championship
65	-	27	8/5/57	London	Ireland	5–1	World Cup Qualifier
66	-	27	15/5/57	Copenhagen	Denmark	4–1	World Cup Qualifier
67	-	27	19/5/57	Dublin	Ireland	1–1	World Cup Qualifier
68	1	28	19/10/57	Cardiff	Wales	4–0	British Championship
69	-	28	27/11/57	London	France	4–0	
70	-	28	19/4/58	Glasgow	Scotland	4–0	British Championship
71	-	28	7/5/58	London	Portugal	2–1	
72	-	28	11/5/58	Belgrade	Yugoslavia	0–5	
73	-	28	18/5/58	Moscow	Soviet Union	1–1	
74	1	29	8/6/58	Gothenburg	Soviet Union	2–2	World Cup
75	1	30	4/10/58	Belfast	N. Ireland	3–3	British Championship
76	-	30	22/10/58	London	Soviet Union	5–0	

PNE TIMELINE

1863: PNE existed as a cricket club.

1875: Preston North End cricket club took a lease on a field at Deepdale, despite financial problems.

1877: In order to combat the financial difficulties which had arisen, PNE turned to rugby in a move that would ultimately fail due to overwhelming competition from already established sides.

1878: PNE played their first game of football but lost 1–0 to Eagley at Deepdale on 5 October.

1880: PNE chose football in order to solve the financial difficulties that they were experiencing (proposed by Mr Harry Carmel and seconded by William Charnley).

1883: Manager William Sudell bought players from Scotland including Ross, Drummond, Russell and Gordon.

1884: West Ham accused Preston of professionalism – that they were paying their players – following an FA Cup tie. PNE were excluded from the competition and Sudell began the move to legalise 'professionalism'. James Ross and Sam Thomson subsequently signed, as did Robert Howarth.

1885/86: PNE went undefeated for 64 games between 22 April 1885 and 26 April 1886, winning 59 of those matches.

1886: Centre forward John Goodall signed and PNE's 'Invincibles' side took shape.

1887/88: PNE won 42 consecutive matches but were beaten 2–1 by West Brom in the 1888 FA Cup final.

1888: PNE became founder members of the Football League.

1888: PNE played their first league game v Burnley, winning 5–2 on 8 September.

1888–89: The club became first ever league winners and completed a league and cup double, having beaten Wolves 3–0 in the final (30/3/1889).

1889–90: The club won their second consecutive league title.

1890/91, 1891/92, 1892/93: PNE finished as league runners-up.

1893: PNE limited company was created and as such William Sudell's time at the helm of the club came to an end.

1900/01: Relegated from Division One (old).

1903/04: Promoted from Division Two (old), having finished top of the table.

1911–15: The 'yo-yo' years as PNE were relegated in 1911/12 and promoted in 1912/13 only to be relegated again in 1913/14 and promoted again in 1914/15.

1922: Huddersfield beat Preston 1–0 in the 1922
FA Cup final on 29 April, Smith scoring a
67th-minute penalty.

1924: Joe McCall, who had played for the club for 20
seasons, retired.

1924/25: PNE relegated to old Division Two.

1933/34: PNE secured promotion to Division One as
J.I. Taylor's management committee brought a
number of talented players to Deepdale.
These included Holdcroft, Lowe and
Shankly.

1937: PNE were beaten 3–1 in the FA Cup final by
Sunderland on 1 May. O'Donnell had put PNE
1–0 up at half time but goals from Gurney, Carter
and Burbanks won Sunderland the game.

1938: Preston beat Huddersfield 1–0 in the FA Cup
final on 30 April. The winning goal was the
first penalty ever awarded at Wembley and was
scored in the 119th minute of the game by George
Mutch.

1938: PNE lost 2–1 to Arsenal in the FA Charity Shield
on 26 September.

1948/49: Club relegated to Division Two.

1950/51: Preston promoted back to Division One.

1952/53: PNE finished runners-up in the league to
Arsenal by a goal difference of 1.

1954: West Brom beat Preston 3–2 in the FA Cup final on 1 May. Goals from Morrison and Wayman were the only consolation as Allan's brace and a Griffin goal won West Brom the game.

1960: Club legend Tom Finney retired.

1960/61: PNE were relegated to Division Two.

1964: PNE lost 3–2 to West Ham in the FA Cup final on 2 May. Preston were 2–1 up with only minutes remaining after Holden and Dawson had scored, but Hurst (89) and Boyce (90) added to Sissons' earlier goal to turn the result around in the Hammers' favour.

1969/70: Club were relegated to the old Division Three only to bounce back to Division Two a season later (1970/71).

1973/74: The club were again relegated to the old Division Three.

1977/78: PNE promoted back to Division Two.

1980/81: Club relegated to Division Three.

1984/85: Preston reached an all-time low after being relegated to Division Four.

1986/87: Preston promoted to old Division Three.

1989: PNE finished 6th in the league but lost 4–2 on aggregate in the play-off semi-final v Port Vale.

1992/93: The leagues were renamed and Preston were then relegated from the new Division Two (old Division Three) back down to Division Three (old Division Four).

1993/94: PNE beat Torquay 4–3 on aggregate in play-off semi-final but lost 4–2 to Wycombe in the final (28/5/1994).

1994/95: Preston lost 2–0 on aggregate against Bury in the play-off semi-finals.

1995/96: PNE were promoted as champions of Division Three and the Sir Tom Finney Stand was opened at Deepdale.

1998: The Bill Shankly Kop stand (formerly the Spion Kop stand) was completed.

1998/99: PNE lost 2–1 on aggregate to Gillingham in the play-off semi-finals.

1999/2000: Club promoted to Division One.

2000/01: Preston reached the Championship play-offs and beat Birmingham in the play-off semi-finals, but lost 3–0 to Bolton Wanderers in the final (28/5/2001).

2001/02: The Allan Kelly Town End was completed.

October 2002: Bryan Gray ended a 7-year stay as PNE Chairman and current Chairman Derek Shaw took over in an interim role.

June 2003: 'Friends of Preston North End', a company owned by now PNE Chairman Shaw, bought the remaining shares of Baxi Partnership.

2004/05: PNE beat Derby County 2–0 on aggregate in the play-off semi-finals but lost 1–0 against West Ham in the final on 30 May.

2005/06: PNE lost 3–1 on aggregate to Leeds United in the play-off semi-finals.

March 2007: David Nugent became the first PNE player since Tom Finney to represent England as he scored in the 3–0 win over Andorra.

June 2007: Nugent was sold for a record fee of £6m to Portsmouth.

16/8/2008: The Invincibles Pavilion was opened.

2008/09: PNE lost 2–1 on aggregate to Sheffield United in the play-off semi-finals.

DAVID NUGENT: PNE LEGEND

Nationality: English
Date of Birth: 2 May 1985
Position: Striker
Period: 2005–7
Appearances: 94
Goals: 33
Joined: From Bury for £100,000
Left: To Portsmouth for £6m

David Nugent, a product of the Liverpool youth academy, spent only two years at Deepdale but made his mark with the sheer number of goals he scored while with PNE. Having debuted in the Football League for Bury, aged only 16, big things were always expected of Nugent and yet it wasn't until Preston captured his signature in 2005, for a fee of £100,000, that he truly shone. Despite interest from both Northampton and Burnley, Nugent moved to Deepdale and scored 33 goals in 94 games. He was unable, however, to help the Lilywhites gain promotion and in 2006 was a member of the squad which lost to Leeds United in the play-off semi finals.

Nugent was a consistent performer for the England under-21s before making his senior England debut on the 28 March 2007 against Andorra. The striker was the first North Ender to play for England since Sir Tom Finney 49 years earlier, and in typical style, he scored a poacher's goal in the 93rd minute of the game. Nugent hasn't appeared for England since but joked after the game about his 100 per cent goalscoring record of one game, one goal.

Following his excellent form in the Championship for Preston, Nugent attracted the interest of Premier League side Portsmouth and was sold for £6m, a record fee received by the club. He never really established himself in Harry Redknapp's side and despite being a member of the 2008 FA Cup-winning squad, Nugent left Portsmouth for a loan spell at fellow Premier League outfit Burnley. There he regained some of his goalscoring form but couldn't prevent Burnley's relegation from England's top fight.

BLOODY PLAY-OFFS ...

Eight attempts, eight failures . . . when it comes to the play-offs, North End fans could be forgiven for feeling a shudder down their spine. The Lilywhites have made the play-offs on eight occasions in three different tiers of English football, but spectacularly failed to achieve the ultimate target of promotion.

The first disappointment came in 1989 when North End lost to Port Vale in the semi-finals. The first leg at Deepdale ended 1–1 but a Darren Beckford hat-trick saw Vale triumph 3–1 in the return and the Potteries side went on to win the final against Bristol Rovers.

It would be another five years before Preston featured again in the play-offs, but the end result was no more pleasing. North End first had to beat Torquay in the semis and after losing the first leg at Plainmoor 2–0, it looked as though another final would pass by – but a dramatic 4–1 win at Deepdale set up a final against Wycombe Wanderers at Wembley, but in front of more than 40,000, Wycombe triumphed 4–2 to win promotion.

A year later and more misery as Bury won both semi-final legs 1–0, firstly at Deepdale and then at Gigg Lane to progress to the final where they in turn lost 2–0 to Chesterfield.

The fourth installment of misery was four years later when Gillingham edged the semi-final to rob the Lilywhites of a money-spinning Wembley final against Manchester City which, incidentally, City won on penalties in front of almost 77,000 fans.

Following promotion to the First Division in 1999/2000, North End reached the play-offs at the first attempt as they attempted to win back-to-back promotions to the Premier League. After beating Birmingham City in the semis on penalties, Bolton awaited in the final but

Wanderers cruised back to the Premier league 3–0 on a miserable day for PNE at the Millennium Stadium.

Then, in 2005, North End choked yet again when the lure of top-flight riches awaited. After beating Derby County in the semi-final, PNE were beaten by West Ham in Cardiff after Bobby Zamora sent half of the 70,000 crowd wild.

Preston's 2006 play-off campaign again resulted in defeat, this time at the semi-final stage against Leeds United – North End fans wondered if there was some kind of curse on the club who were clearly jinxed when it came to the dread POs.

In 2009, Preston fans wondered if, finally, the hex was about to end. After overtaking Cardiff City on the final day of the season, the Lilywhites faced Sheffield United over two legs in the semis. A 1–1 draw at Deepdale swung the pendulum the Blades' way and so it proved, with the hosts winning 1–0 at Bramall Lane. It has to end – one day . . .

PNE FA CUP FINALS

Preston North End have reached the final of English football's most famous cup competition on seven occasions, and have managed to bring the trophy back to Lancashire twice. In 1888 Preston suffered defeat at the hands of West Brom going down 2–1 to the Baggies. However, it did not take long for the Lilywhites to get their hands on the silverware when they were victorious the following season. Goals from Dewhurst, Ross and Thompson gave the club a 3–0 win over another team from the Black Country in the form of Wolves; this completed a great double as PNE had also won the league that year. Thirty-three years went by before the club made another appearance in the final, but lost out 1–0 due to a penalty against Huddersfield at Stamford Bridge in what was to be the last final played before the opening of Wembley. Another loss was inflicted in 1937 when Sunderland got the better of PNE by coming out on top 3–1. The club was seemingly spurred on by this loss, as they returned to Wembley the following year but this time with a more positive outcome. In the final minute of extra-time against Huddersfield, North End were awarded a penalty which was duly dispatched by Georg Mutch which gained revenge for the 1922 final loss against the Yorkshiremen. This was to be the club's final triumph in the competition, although the Lilywhites reached the last round on two more occasions in 1954 and '64 which they lost to West Brom and West Ham respectively. Preston North End have not won the trophy in over 70 years.

ASSOCIATE MEMBERS' CUP (JOHNSTONE'S PAINT/AUTO WINDSCREENS, ETC.)

As a club, Preston have never enjoyed too much success in this competition that is more famous for its continuous changing of sponsors than the eventual winners of the trophy each year. The closest the club have come to reaching the final was getting to the 'Northern Section' final on two different occasions only to suffer defeat in the two-legged ties. In the 1987/88 season the club made it to the regional final where they came up against Burnley. The tie was drawn up to the end of the second set of 90 minutes, but then Burnley found something extra and dumped out the Whites with two goals in extra time. Again, in 1990/91, a similar fate was suffered, but this time at the hands of Tranmere Rovers. However, the result was far more comprehensive following a 4–0 victory in the first leg for the Wirral side who eventually went on to win 4–1 on aggregate.

TEXACO/ANGLO-SCOTTISH CUP

Preston made three appearances in the trophy between 1978 and 1981. Unfortunately, they had limited success, winning only one game during their first foray into the competition. Comparatively, their second attempt was more pleasing for the fans as they made it through the group stages. However, they lost out in the two-legged quarter-final to Morton 5–1 on aggregate. In the final year of the tournament, Preston only managed a solitary point, and therefore didn't make it out of the group stages.

FA YOUTH CUP

Preston have once managed to reach the final of this competition which pits the youngsters of each English club against each other to see who has the most promising stars of the future. In 1960, a side that included the likes of John Barton, Johnny Hart, David Will, George Ross, Dave Wilson, Rodney Webb and Michael Smith made it to the final where they came up against a strong Chelsea outfit. For the game at Deepdale 27,000 people turned out to watch the young prodigies, but were unable to cheer them to victory as they lost 4–1 on the night and 5–2 on aggregate.

PNE FA CUP COMPLETE RECORD

1883/84

r1				bye
r2	Great Lever	home	W	4–1
r3	Eagley	home	W	9–1
r4	Upton Park	home	D	1–1

1885/86

r1	Great Lever	W/o		
r2	Astley Bridge	home	W	11–3
r3	Bolton Wanderers	away	W	3–2

(Bolton Wanderers handed victory – Preston disqualified)

1886/87

r1	Queen's Park	away	W	3–0
r2	Witton Albion	home	W	6–0
r3	Renton	neutral	W	2–0
r4				bye
r5	Old Foresters	away	W	3–0
r6	Old Carthusians	away	W	2–1 (aet)
sf	WBA	neutral	L	1–3

1887/88

r1	Hyde	home	W	26–0
r2	Bolton Wanderers	home	W	9–1
r2	Everton	home	W	6–1
				(match void)
r3	Halliwell	home	W	4–0
r4				bye
r5	Aston Villa	away	W	3–1
r6	Sheffield Wednesday	away	W	3–1
sf	Crewe Alexandra	neutral	W	4–0
f	WBA	neutral	L	1–2

1888/89

r1	Bootle (old)	away	W	3–0
r2	Grimsby Town	away	W	2–0
r3	Birmingam St George	home	W	2–0
sf	WBA	neutral	W	1–0
f	Wolves	neutral	W	3–0

1889/90

r1	Manchester Utd	home	W	6–1
r2	Lincoln City	home	W	4–0
r3	Bolton Wanderers	home	L	2–3

1890/91

r1	Stoke City	away	L	0–3

1891/92

r1	M'boro Ironopolis	home	W	6–0
r2	Middlesbrough	away	W	2–1
r3	Nottingham Forest	away	L	0–2

1892/93

r1	Burton United	home	W	9–2
r2	Accrington	away	W	4–1
r3	M'boro Ironopolis	home	D	2–2
r3r	M'boro Ironopolis	away	W	7–0
sf	Everton	neutral	D	2–2
sfr	Everton	neutral	D	0–0
sfr2	Everton	neutral	L	1–2

1893/84

r1	Reading	home	W	18–0
r2	Liverpool	away	L	2–3

1894/95

r1	Luton Town	away	W	2–0
r2	Sunderland	away	L	0–2

1895/96

r1	Sunderland	away	L	1–4

1896/97

r1	Manchester City	home	W	6–0
r2	Stoke City	home	W	2–1
r3	Aston Villa	home	D	1–1
r3r	Aston Villa	away	D	0–0
r3r2	Aston Villa	neutral	L	2–3

1897/98

r1	Newcastle United	home	L	1–2

1898/99

r1	Grimsby Town	home	W	7–0
r2	Sheffield United	home	D	2–2
r2r	Sheffield United	away	L	1–2

1899/1900

r1	Tottenham Hotspur	home	W	1–0
r2	Blackburn Rovers	home	W	1–0
r3	Nottm Forest	home	D	0–0
r3r	Nottm Forest	away	L	0–1

1900/01

r1	Tottenham Hotspur	away	D	1–1
r1r	Tottenham Hotspur	home	L	2–4

1901/02

r1	Manchester City	away	D	1–1
r1r	Manchester City	home	D	0–0 aet
r1r2	Manchester City	home	L	2–4 aet

1902/03

ir	Bishop Auckland	away	W	3–1
r1	Manchester City	home	W	3–1
r2	Millwall	away	L	1–4

1903/04

ir	Darwen	home	W	2–1
r1	Grimsby Town	home	W	1–0
r2	Middlesbrough	home	L	0–3

1904/05

r1	Derby County	away	W	2–0
r2	Bristol City	away	D	0–0
r2r	Bristol City	home	W	1–0
r3	Sheffield Wednesday	home	D	1–1
r3r	Sheffield Wednesday	away	L	0–3

1905/06

r1	Birmingham City	away	L	0–1

1906/07

r1	Notts County	away	L	0–1

1907/08

r1	Brighton & H A	away	D	1–1
r1r	Brighton & H A	home	D	1–1
r1r2	Brighton & H A	neutral	L	0–1

1908/09

r1	Middlesbrough	home	W	1–0
r2	Sunderland	home	L	1–2

1909/10

r1	Coventry City	home	L	1–2

1910/11

r1	Brentford	away	W	1–0
r2	West Ham United	away	L	0–3

1911/12

r1	Manchester City	home	L	0–1

1912/13
r1	Plymouth Argyle	away	L	0–2

1913/14
r1	Bristol Rovers	home	W	5–2
r2	Glossop North End	away	W	1–0
r3	Sunderland	away	L	0–2

1914/15
r1	Manchester City	home	D	0–0
r1r	Manchester City	away	L	0–3

(1915 to 1919 no competition owing to First World War)

1919/20
r1	Stockport County	home	W	3–1
r2	Blackpool	home	W	2–1
r3	Bradford City	home	L	0–3

1920/21
r1	Bolton Wanderers	home	W	2–0
r2	Watford	home	W	4–1
r3	Luton Town	away	W	3–2
r4	Hull City	away	D	0–0
r4r	Hull City	home	W	1–0
sf	Tottenham Hotspur	neutral	L	1–2

1921/22
r1	Wolves	home	W	3–0
r2	Newcastle United	home	W	3–1
r3	Barnsley	away	D	1–1
r3r	Barnsley	home	W	3–0
r4	Arsenal	away	D	1–1
r4r	Arsenal	home	W	2–1 aet
sf	Tottenham Hotspur	neutral	W	2–1
f	Huddersfield Town	neutral	L	0–1

1922/23

r1	Aberdare Athletic	away	W	3–1
r2	Charlton Athletic	away	L	0–2

1923/24

r1	Everton	away	L	1–3

1924/25

r1	Manchester City	home	W	4–1
r2	WBA	away	L	0–2

1925/26

r3	Blackburn Rovers	away	D	1–1
r3r	Blackburn Rovers	home	L	1–4

1926/27

r3	Lincoln City	away	W	4–2
r4	Middlesbrough	home	L	0–3

1927/28

r3	Everton	home	L	0–3

1928/29

r3	Watford	away	L	0–1

1929/30

r3	Portsmouth	away	L	0–2

1930/31

r3	Tottenham Hotspur	away	L	1–3

1931/32

r3	Bolton Wanderers	home	D	0–0
r3r	Bolton Wanderers	away	W	5–2
r4	Wolves	home	W	2–0
r5	Huddersfield Town	away	L	0–4

1932/33
r3	Birmingham City	away	L	1–2

1933/34
r3	Leeds United	away	W	1–0
r4	Workington	away	W	2–1
r5	Northampton Town	home	W	4–0
r6	Leicester City	home	L	0–1

1934/35
r3	Barnsley	home	D	0–0
r3r	Barnsley	away	W	1–0
r4	Swindon Town	away	W	2–0
r5	Bristol City	away	D	0–0
r5r	Bristol City	home	W	5–0
r6	WBA	away	L	0–1

1935/36
r3	Everton	away	W	3–1
r4	Sheffield United	home	D	0–0
r4r	Sheffield United	away	L	0–2

1936/37
r3	Newcastle United	home	W	2–0
r4	Stoke City	home	W	5–1
r5	Exeter City	home	W	5–3
r6	Tottenham Hotspur	away	W	3–1
sf	WBA	neutral	W	4–1
f	Sunderland	neutral	L	1–3

1937/38
r3	West Ham United	home	W	3–0
r4	Leicester City	home	W	2–0
r5	Arsenal	away	W	1–0
r6	Brentford	away	W	3–0

sf	Aston Villa	neutral	W	2–1
f	Huddersfield Town	neutral	W	1–0 aet

1938/39

r3	Runcorn Halton	away	W	4–2
r4	Aston Villa	home	W	2–0
r5	Newcastle United	away	W	2–1
r6	Portsmouth	away	L	0–1

(1939 to 1945 no competition owing to Second World War)

1945/46

r3 (1)	Everton	home	W	2–1
r3 (2)	Everton	away	D	2–2
				aet (4–3)
r4 (1)	Manchester United	away	L	0–1
r4 (2)	Manchester United	home	W	3–1
				(3–2)
r5 (1)	Charlton Athletic	home	D	1–1
r5 (2)	Charlton Athletic	away	L	0–6
				(7–1)

1946/47

r3	Northampton Town	away	W	2–1
r4	Barnsley	home	W	6–0
r5	Sheffield Wednesday	away	W	2–0
r6	Charlton Athletic	away	L	1–2

1947/48

r3	Millwall	away	W	2–1
r4	Portsmouth	away	W	3–1
r5	Manchester City	away	W	1–0
r6	Manchester United	away	L	1–4

1948/49

r3	Mansfield Town	home	W	2–1
r4	Leicester City	away	L	0–2

1949/50

r3	Watford	away	D	2–2
r3r	Watford	home	L	0–1

1950/51

r3	Leicester City	away	W	3–0
r4	Huddersfield Town	home	L	0–2

1951/52

r3	Bristol Rovers	away	L	0–2

1952/53

r3	Wolves	home	W	5–2
r4	Tottenham Hotspur	home	D	2–2
r4r	Tottenham Hotspur	away	L	0–1

1953/54

r3	Derby County	away	W	2–0
r4	Lincoln City	away	W	2–0
r5	Ipswich Town	home	W	6–1
r6	Leicester City	away	D	1–1
r6r	Leicester City	home	D	2–2 aet
r6r2	Leicester City	neutral	W	3–1
sf	Sheffield Wednesday	neutral	W	2–0
f	WBA	neutral	L	2–3

1954/55

r3	Fulham	away	W	3–2
r4	Sunderland	home	D	3–3
r4r	Sunderland	away	L	0–2

1955/56

r3	West Ham United	away	L	2–5

1956/57

r3	Sheffield Wednesday	home	D	0–0
r3r	Sheffield Wednesday	away	D	2–2 aet
r3r2	Sheffield Wednesday	neutral	W	5–1
r4	Bristol Rovers	away	W	4–1
r5	Arsenal	home	D	3–3
r5r	Arsenal	away	L	1–2

1957/58

r3	Bolton Wanderers	home	L	0–3

1958/59

r3	Derby County	away	D	2–2
r3r	Derby County	home	W	4–2 aet
r4	Bradford City	home	W	3–2
r5	Bolton Wanderers	away	D	2–2
r5r	Bolton Wanderers	home	D	1–1 aet
r5r2	Bolton Wanderers	neutral	L	0–1

1959/60

r3	Stoke City	away	D	1–1
r3r	Stoke City	home	W	3–1
r4	Bristol Rovers	away	D	3–3
r4r	Bristol Rovers	home	W	5–1
r5	Brighton & H A	home	W	2–1
r6	Aston Villa	away	L	0–2

1960/61

r3	Accrington Stanley	home	D	1–1
r3r	Accrington Stanley	away	W	4–0
r4	Swansea Town	away	L	1–2

1961/62

r3	Watford	home	W	3–2
r4	Weymouth	home	W	2–0
r5	Liverpool	away	D	0–0
r5r	Liverpool	home	D	0–0 aet
r5r2	Liverpool	neutral	W	1–0
r6	Manchester United	home	D	0–0
r6r	Manchester United	away	L	1–2

1962/63

r3	Sunderland	home	L	1–4

1963/64

r3	Nottingham Forest	away	D	0–0
r3r	Nottingham Forest	home	W	1–0
r4	Bolton Wanderers	away	D	2–2
r4r	Bolton Wanderers	home	W	2–1
r5	Carlisle United	home	W	1–0
r6	Oxford United	away	W	2–1
sf	Swansea Town	neutral	W	2–1
f	West Ham United	neutral	L	2–3

1964/65

r3	Barnet	away	W	3–2
r4	Bolton Wanderers	home	L	1–2

1965/66

r3	Charlton Athletic	away	W	3–2
r4	Bolton Wanderers	away	D	1–1
r4r	Bolton Wanderers	home	W	3–2
r5	Tottenham Hotspur	home	W	2–1
r6	Manchester United	home	D	1–1
r6r	Manchester United	away	L	1–3

1966/67

r3	Aston Villa	home	L	0–1

1967/68

r3	QPR	away	W	3–1
r4	Tottenham Hotspur	away	L	1–3

1968/69

r3	Nottingham Forest	home	W	3–0
r4	Chelsea	home	D	0–0
r4r	Chelsea	away	L	1–2

1969/70

r3	Derby County	home	D	1–1
r3r	Derby County	away	L	1–4

1970/71

r1	Chester City	home	D	1–1
r1r	Chester City	away	L	0–1

1971/72

r3	Bristol City	home	W	4–2
r4	Manchester United	home	L	0–2

1972/73

r3	Grimsby Town	away	D	0–0
r3r	Grimsby Town	home	L	0–1

1973/74

r3	Fulham	away	L	0–1

1974/75

r1	Blyth Spartans	away	D	1–1
r1r	Blyth Spartans	home	W	5–1
r2	Bishop Auckland	away	W	2–0
r3	Carlisle United	home	L	0–1

1975/76

r1	Scunthorpe United	home	W	2–1
r2	Scarborough	away	L	2–3

1976/77

r1	Crewe Alexandra	away	D	1–1
r1r	Crewe Alexandra	home	D	2–2 aet
r1r2	Crewe Alexandra	neutral	W	3–0
r2	Halifax Town	away	L	0–1

1977/78

r1	Lincoln City	home	W	3–2
r2	Wrexham	home	L	0–2

1978/79

r3	Derby County	home	W	3–0
r4	Southampton	home	L	0–1

1979/80

r3	Ipswich Town	home	L	0–3

1980/81

r3	Bristol Rovers	home	L	3–4

1981/82

r1	Chesterfield	away	L	1–4

1982/83

r1	Shepshed Charterhouse	home	W	5–1
r2	Blackpool	home	W	2–1
r3	Leeds United	away	L	0–3

1983/84

r1	Scunthorpe United	away	L	0–1

1984/85

r1	Bury	home	W	4–3
r2	Telford United	home	L	1–4

1985/86

r1	Walsall	away	L	3–7

1986/87

r1	Bury	home	W	5–1
r2	Chorley	neutral	D	0–0
r2r	Chorley	home	W	5–0
r3	Middlesbrough	away	W	1–0
r4	Newcastle United	away	L	0–2

1987/88

r1	Mansfield Town	home	D	1–1
r1r	Mansfield Town	away	L	2–4

1988/89

r1	Tranmere Rovers	home	D	1–1
r1r	Tranmere Rovers	away	L	0–3

1989/90

r1	Tranmere Rovers	home	W	1–0
r2	Whitley Bay	away	L	0–2

1990/91

r1	Mansfield Town	home	L	0–1

1991/92

r1	Mansfield Town	away	D	1–1
r1r	Mansfield Town	away	W	1–0
r2	Witton Albion	home	W	5–1
r3	Sheffield Wednesday	home	L	0–2

1992/93

r1	Bradford City	away	D	1–1
r1r	Bradford City	home	L	4–5

1993/94

r1	Mansfield Town	away	W	2–1
r2	Shrewsbury Town	away	W	1–0
r3	Bournemouth	home	W	2–1
r4	Kidderminster Harriers	away	L	0–1

1994/95

r1	Blackpool	home	W	1–0
r2	Walsall	home	D	1–1
r2r	Walsall	away	L	0–4

1995/96

r1	Carlisle United	away	W	2–1
r2	Bradford City	away	L	1–2

1996/97

r1	Altrincham	home	W	4–1
r2	York City	home	L	2–3

1997/98

r1	Doncaster Rovers	home	W	3–2
r2	Notts County	home	D	2–2
r2r	Notts County	away	W	2–1
r3	Stockport County	home	L	1–2

1998/99

r1	Ford United	home	W	3–0
r2	Walsall	home	W	2–0
r3	Arsenal	home	L	2–4

1999/2000

r1	Bristol Rovers	away	W	1–0
r2	Enfield	home	D	0–0
r2r	Enfield	away	W	0–3
r3	Oldham Athletic	home	W	2–1
r4	Plymouth Argyle	away	W	3–0
r5	Everton	away	L	0–2

2000/01

r3	Stockport County	home	L	0–1

2001/02

r3	Brighton & H A	away	W	2–0
r4	Sheffield United	home	W	2–1
r5	Chelsea	away	L	1–3

2002/03

r3	Rochdale	home	L	1–2

2003/04

r3	Reading	home	D	3–3
r3r	Reading	away	W	2–1
r4	Swansea City	away	L	1–2

2004/05

r3	WBA	away	L	0–2

2005/06

r3	Crewe Alexandra	home	W	2–1
r4	Crystal Palace	home	D	1–1
r4r	Crystal Palace	away	W	2–1
r5	Middlesbrough	home	L	0–2

2006/07

r3	Sunderland	home	W	1–0
r4	Crystal Palace	away	W	2–0
r5	Manchester City	home	L	1–3

2007/08

r3	Scunthorpe United	home	W	1–0
r4	Derby County	away	W	4–1
r5	Portsmouth	home	L	0–1

2008/09

r3	Liverpool	home	L	0–2

2009/10

r3	Colchester United	home	W	7–0
r4	Chelsea	home	L	0–2

LEAGUE CUP COMPLETE RECORD

1960/61

r1	Peterborough United	home	W	4–1
r2	Gillingham	away	D	1–1
r2r	Gillingham	home	W	3–0
r3	Aston Villa	home	D	3–3
r3r	Aston Villa	away	L	1–3

1961/62

r1	Aldershot	home	W	3–1
r2	Swindon Town	home	W	3–1
r3	Rotherham United	home	D	0–0
r3r	Rotherham United	away	L	0–3

1962/63

r2	QPR	away	W	2–1
r3	Northampton Town	away	D	1–1
r3r	Northampton Town	home	W	2–1
r4	Aston Villa	away	L	2–6

1963/64

r2	Newcastle United	away	L	0–3

1964/65

r2	Doncaster Rovers	away	L	0–1

1965/66

r2	Plymouth Argyle	home	W	1–0
r3	Huddersfield Town	away	W	1–0
r4	Grimsby Town	away	L	0–4

1966/67

r2	Crewe Alexandra	home	W	2–0
r3	Leeds United	home	D	1–1
r3r	Leeds United	away	L	0–3

1967/68

r2	Oxford United	away	L	1–2

1968/69

r1	Oldham Athletic	home	D	1–1
r1r	Oldham Athletic	away	W	1–0
r2	Crystal Palace	away	L	1–3

1969/70

r1	Bury	home	L	0–1

1970/71

r1	Stockport County	away	W	1–0
r2	Torquay United	away	W	3–1
r3	WBA	home	L	0–1

1971/72

r1	Barrow	away	W	2–0
r2	Tranmere Rovers	away	W	1–0
r3	Watford	away	D	1–1
r3r	Watford	home	W	2–1
r4	Tottenham Hotspur	away	D	1–1
r4r	Tottenham Hotspur	home	L	1–2 aet

1972/73

r1	Workington	away	L	0–1

1973/74

r1	Bolton Wanderers	away	D	1–1
r1r	Bolton Wanderers	home	L	0–2 aet

1974/75

r1	Rochdale	home	W	1–0
r2	Sunderland	home	W	2–0
r3	Chester City	away	L	0–1

1975/76

r1 (1)	Blackburn Rovers	home	W	2–0
r1 (2)	Blackburn Rovers	away	D	0–0
				(2–0)
r2	Hull City	away	L	2–4

1976/77

r1 (1)	Bury	away	L	1–2
r1 (2)	Bury	home	D	1–1
				(2–3)

1977/78

r1 (1)	Port Vale	away	L	1–2
r1 (2)	Port Vale	home	W	2–1
				(3–3)
r1r	Port Vale	neutral	W	2–1
r2	Walsall	away	D	0–0
r2r	Walsall	home	L	0–1 aet

1978/79

r1 (1)	Huddersfield Town	home	W	3–0
r1 (2)	Huddersfield Town	away	D	2–2
				(5–2)
r2	QPR	home	L	1–3

1979/80

r2 (1)	Birmingham City	away	L	1–2 aet
r2 (2)	Birmingham City	home	L	0–1
				(1–3)

1980/81

r2 (1)	Wigan Athletic	home	W	1–0
r2 (2)	Wigan Athletic	away	W	2–1
				(3–1)
r3	Oxford United	home	W	1–0
r4	WBA	away	D	0–0
r4r	WBA	home	D	1–1 aet
r4r2	WBA	away	L	1–2 aet

1981/82

r1 (1)	Halifax Town	away	W	2–1
r1 (2)	Halifax Town	home	D	0–0
				(2–1)
r2 (1)	Leicester City	home	W	1–0
r2 (2)	Leicester City	away	L	0–4
				(1–4)

1982/83

r1 (1)	Walsall	away	W	1–0
r1 (2)	Walsall	home	D	1–1
				(2–1)
r2 (1)	Norwich City	away	L	1–2
r2 (2)	Norwich City	home	L	1–2
				(2–4)

1983/84

r1 (1)	Tranmere Rovers	home	W	1–0
r1 (2)	Tranmere Rovers	away	D	0–0
				(1–0)
r2 (1)	Wolves	away	W	3–2
r2 (2)	Wolves	home	W	1–0
				(4–2)
r3	Sheffield Wednesday	home	L	0–2

1984/85

r1 (1)	Tranmere Rovers	away	W	3–2
r1 (2)	Tranmere Rovers	home	D	2–2
				(5–4) aet
r2 (1)	Norwich City	home	D	3–3
r2 (2)	Norwich City	away	L	1–6
				(4–9)

1985/86

r1 (1)	Blackpool	home	W	2–1
r1 (2)	Blackpool	away	W	3–1
				(5–2)
r2 (1)	Norwich City	home	D	1–1
r2 (2)	Norwich City	away	L	1–2
				(2–3)

1986/87

r1 (1)	Blackpool	away	D	0–0
r1 (2)	Blackpool	home	W	2–1
				(2–1)
r2 (1)	West Ham United	home	D	1–1
r2 (2)	West Ham United	away	L	1–4
				(2–5)

1987/88

r1 (1)	Bury	away	D	2–2
r1 (2)	Bury	home	L	2–3
				(4–5) aet

1988/89

r1 (1)	Wigan Athletic	away	D	0–0
r1 (2)	Wigan Athletic	home	W	1–0
				(1–0)
r2 (1)	Norwich City	away	L	0–2
r2 (2)	Norwich City	home	L	0–3
				(0–5)

1989/90

r1 (1)	Tranmere Rovers	home	L	3–4
r1 (2)	Tranmere Rovers	away	L	1–3
				(4–7)

1990/91

r1 (1)	Chester City	home	W	2–0
r1 (2)	Chester City	away	L	1–5
				(3–5)

1991/92

r1 (1)	Scarborough	home	W	5–4
r1 (2)	Scarborough	away	L	1–3
				(6–7)

1992/93

r1 (1)	Stoke City	home	W	2–1
r1 (2)	Stoke City	away	L	0–4
				(2–5)

1993/94

r1 (1)	Burnley	home	L	1–2
r1 (2)	Burnley	away	L	1–4
				(2–6)

1994/95

r1 (1)	Stockport County	home	D	1–1
r1 (2)	Stockport County	away	L	1–4
				(2–5)

1995/96

r1 (1)	Sunderland	home	D	1–1
r1 (2)	Sunderland	away	L	2–3
				(3–4)

1996/97

r1 (1)	Wigan Athletic	away	W	3–2
r1 (2)	Wigan Athletic	home	D	4–4
				(7–6)
r2 (1)	Tottenham Hotspur	home	D	1–1
r2 (2)	Tottenham Hotspur	away	L	0–3

1997/98

r1 (1)	Rotherham United	away	W	3–1
r1 (2)	Rotherham United	home	W	2–0
				(5–1)
r2 (1)	Blackburn Rovers	away	L	0–6
r2 (2)	Blackburn Rovers	home	W	1–0
				(1–6)

1998/99

r1 (1) Grimsby Town	away	D	0–0
r1 (2) Grimsby Town	home	D	0–0
			(lost on pens)

1999/2000

r1 (1) Wrexham	home	W	1–0
r1 (2) Wrexham	away	W	2–0
			(3–0)
r2 (1) Sheffield United	away	L	0–2
r2 (2) Sheffield United	home	W	3–0
			(3–2)
r3 Arsenal	away	L	1–2

2000/01

r1 (1) Shrewsbury Town	away	L	0–1
r1 (2) Shrewsbury Town	home	W	4–1
			(4–2)
r2 (1) Coventry City	home	L	1–3
r2 (2) Coventry City	away	L	1–4
			(2–7)

2001/02

r1 Kidderminster Harriers	away	W	3–2
r2 Tranmere Rovers	away	L	1–4

2002/03

r1 Scunthorpe United	home	W	2–1 aet
r2 Macclesfield Town	away	W	2–1
r3 Birmingham City	away	W	2–0
r4 Aston Villa	away	L	0–5

2003/04

r1 Notts County	home	D	0–0
			(lost on pens)

2004/05

r1	Mansfield Town	away	W	4–0
r2	Leicester City	away	W	3–2
r3	Everton	away	L	0–2

2005/06

| r1 | Barnsley | home | D | 2–2 |
| | | | (lost on pens) | |

2006/07

| r1 | Port Vale | away | L | 1–2 |

2007/08

| r1 | Morecambe | home | L | 1–2 |

2008/09

| r1 | Chesterfield | home | W | 2–0 |
| r2 | Derby County | home | L | 0–1 |

2009/10

r1	Morecambe	home	W	5–1
r2	Leicester City	home	W	2–1
r3	Tottenham Hotspur	home	L	1–5

PROMOTION AND RELEGATION

The first time that PNE were relegated was in 1901 when they finished 17th in the First Division. Following three years in the second tier, the club finally gained a return to the top flight by winning the league. In the four seasons prior to the outbreak of the First World War, the Lilywhites were somewhat of a yo-yo club by following each relegation with a promotion back to the

First Division. This sequence included a Second Division title in 1912/13. Having spent the five seasons following the war battling relegation, Preston finally succumbed and were sent back to the second tier in 1925, where they would stay for nine years until moving back up one league in 1934 by finishing as runners-up. Technically, the club were a top-flight side for 15 years, but then along came the Second World War, which resulted in five seasons being lost to the conflict. The Lilywhites dropped down to the Second Division in 1949. However, Preston only spent two campaigns at that level and were subsequently promoted as champions in 1951.

The end of the 1950s and start of the following decade saw a decline in the fortunes of the club both on and off the pitch. Preston dropped down to the second tier in 1961 as they ended up bottom of the First Division, which was a dreadful financial blow to the club and meant that the club's coffers were seriously limited. Due to this lack of money players were forcibly sold and the club was unable to replace them with anyone of similar quality. This continuous demise saw them relegated to the Third Division in 1970 following a decade of mediocrity in England's second tier. Their first adventure into the lowly depths of the Football League only lasted for one year as they won the title to propel them back up. Two seasons of just about keeping their heads above the relegation zone followed, until they eventually went back down in the 1973/74 season.

Preston achieved three mid-table finishes prior to making a successful challenge for promotion in 1978 as the club finished 3rd in the league. 1981 was another season of disappointment as the team were unable to keep their Second Division status as they ended up in 20th place. More seasons of pure disappointment followed as the team struggled in the Third Division, but they managed to survive until 1985 when they were relegated to the bottom tier of English football. The Lilywhites spent two seasons at this level, but their second-place finish in 1987 saw them promoted to the Third Division.

While the league structure was being altered in the 1990s there was to be no change in the fortunes of PNE as they fell from the Second to Third Division in 1993. The subsequent seasons saw two play-off failures until they won the league title in 1996 with 86 points to their name. The most recent promotion for the Lilywhites was in 2000 as they won the Second Division. Since that last title, the club have failed on four different occasions in the play-offs as they attempt to reach the Premier League.

BRIAN MOONEY: PNE LEGEND

Name: Brian Mooney
Position: Midfielder
Career at PNE: 1987–91
Apps: 128
Goals: 26

Dubbed the 'master of plastic' by dedicated North End supporters, Irish winger Brian Mooney spent the best years of his career on Deepdale's artificial turf. Initially scouted by Liverpool while playing in his native Dublin, Mooney moved to Anfield in 1983. Despite this being a dream move for the then seventeen-year-old, the youngster found it hard to break his way into the club's first XI. His performances for Liverpool's reserve side earned him a place in his country's under-21 team and saw him represent the Republic of Ireland in the 1985 World Youth Championship. The Liverpool wide man boasted great pace and skill but even an impressive loan spell at Wrexham couldn't prove to Liverpool that he was worthy of a place beside club legends Ian Rush and Kenny Dalglish, who were playing in the side at the time.

Having made only one appearance for the Merseyside club, Mooney spent a month on loan at Third Division Preston before making the move away from Anfield on a permanent basis in 1987. Preston paid £25,000 for the tricky winger. Playing on Deepdale's artificial surface, the Irishman became a player who could make something from nothing with the ability to beat any defender. Mooney was named the club's official Player of the Year in 1988/89 and was voted second in the BBC's poll to find the club's all time cult hero – runner-up only to club legend Sir Tom Finney.

Despite earning the plaudits from some of England's top managers and reportedly catching the eye of then Ireland manager Jack Charlton, Mooney was never capped by his country. In 1991, Sunderland bought the winger for £225,000. Injury took its toll on Mooney however and at the age of 27, following a loan spell at Burnley, he returned to Ireland where he played for both Shelbourne and Bohemians before drifting out of the game altogether.

KIT COLOURS

The inaugural year of PNE saw the team sporting a horizontally-striped navy and white shirt, but this outfit was to last for only two seasons. A more distinctive kit consisting of red and white halves was produced for the following campaign, but was once again short-lived, being replaced with vertical stripes of the same colours.

However, the attire was once again changed for the first season of the newly formed Football League with the use of a plain white shirt and navy shorts. In this season the club famously won a league and cup double, and owing to the success, Preston decided to keep the lucky colours for good. The simply styled kit also inspired Tottenham's kit design, who copied PNE in the hope that the shirts' success in Lancashire would rub off on the North Londoners. It did!

MATCH ABANDONED

v Weymouth 27 January 1962
FA Cup 4th Round
Only 16 minutes of this tie were played, owing to thick fog. To indicate how bad the weather was the Weymouth keeper was left on the pitch for some time after the ref had cancelled the match, and had to be eventually rescued by his team-mates when they became worried about his whereabouts having not returned to the dressing room! PNE went on to win the replay 2–0.

v Chelsea (a) 29 January 1969
FA Cup 4th Round replay
The match was stopped with a mere 15 minutes of play left, owing to floodlight failure. At the time the Blues were winning 2–0. However, this wasn't much of a reprieve as Chelsea won the 'replay' 2–1 the following week.

CREST

The club badge is based on the city's coat of arms, with the incorporation of the paschal lamb. The animal is the Lamb of St Winifred who is the patron saint of Preston. However, the club omits the letters 'PP' which stand on the city's official crest, and have replaced it with the club's name in order to make it specific to football, while still showing that they represent the country's fiftieth city.

MASCOT: DEEPDALE DUCK

Unfortunately, Preston have been unable to fund a duck house for their mascot and so he has instead made Deepdale his home. The beloved creature is one of the longest-serving mascots in the Football League. He has been a consistent performer at mascot races and is popular within the city, making appearances at a variety of events, including school and hospital visits

BLANKET BLANKS

PNE's first campaign saw the club keep no less than 18 clean sheets out of the 27 games played during the 1888/89 season – a league and cup double season, no less. Burnley breached North End's defence more than any other side with 4 goals out of the 15 conceded in total.

PNE LADIES

The female branch of the Lilywhites was founded in 1971, though originally they were called the Duke of York. Since then they have become very successful in regional league and cup competitions. The club has also played under the name Preston Rangers. Now they are the official women's team of Preston North End and currently have three senior sides.

PNE WFC Honours

Northern Women's Combination League Champions 2005/06

North West WRF League Premier Div Champions 2003/04; 1997/98

North West WRF League Cup Winners 2003/04; 1996/97; 1992/93; 1985/86; 1983/84

North West WRF League Divisional Cup Winners 2003/04; 1994/95; 1993/94

Lancashire FA Women's Challenge Cup Champions 1996/97

WFA Cup semi-finalists 1982/83 and 1989/90

PNE TITLE-WINNING TABLES

Preston North End have won the league on two occasions. It is something supporters are rightly proud of, so here are the final standings of those two historic seasons:

English Division One 1888/89

Team	P	W	D	L	F	A	G/D	Pts
PNE	22	18	4	0	74	15	59	40
Aston Villa	22	12	5	5	61	43	18	29
Wolves	22	12	4	6	50	37	13	28
Blackburn R	22	10	6	6	66	45	21	26
Bolton W	22	10	2	10	63	59	4	22
WBA	22	10	2	10	40	46	-6	22
Accrington	22	6	8	8	48	48	0	20
Everton	22	9	2	11	35	46	-11	20
Burnley	22	7	3	12	42	62	-20	17
Derby Co	22	7	2	13	41	61	-20	16
Notts Coy	22	5	2	15	40	73	-33	12
Stoke City	22	4	4	14	26	51	-25	12

English Division One 1889/90

Team	P	W	D	L	F	A	G/D	Pts
PNE	22	15	3	4	71	30	41	33
Everton	22	14	3	5	65	40	25	31
Blackburn R	22	12	3	7	78	41	37	27
Wolves	22	10	5	7	51	38	13	25
WBA	22	11	3	8	47	50	-3	25
Accrington	22	9	6	7	53	56	-3	24
Derby Co	22	9	3	10	43	55	-12	21
Aston Villa	22	7	5	10	43	51	-8	19
Bolton W	22	9	1	12	54	65	-11	19
Notts Co	22	6	5	11	43	51	-8	17
Burnley	22	4	5	13	36	65	-29	13
Stoke City	22	3	4	15	27	69	-42	10

NOWHERE TO HYDE?

North End racked up their club record victory on 15 October 1887 when Hyde were soundly thrashed 26–0 in the FA Cup 1st round. Jimmy Ross created another club record that is unlikely to be beaten anytime soon by grabbing 7 goals during the romp. For the record, Preston went all the way to the final, only to lose 2–1 to West Bromwich Albion.

THE FIRST OF MANY ...

North End began Football League life on 8 September 1888 in a clash with Lancastrian rivals Burnley at Deepdale. More than 6,000 fans attended the game which kicked off some 50 minutes late owing to the tardiness of the Clarets who didn't turn up on time. PNE went ahead on just two minutes through Fred Dewhurst and went on to win 5–2. Through the annals of time, the fact that Dewhurst's goal came so quickly – the fastest of the day – it has been wrongly accredited at the first ever Football League goal scored. Had the match kicked off on time, it would have been so, but since the other inaugural fixtures were already at half time by the time the Preston game began, it is, sadly, not true.

A PRINCELY VICTORY

In 1997 HRH Prince Charles visited Deepdale during a whistle-stop tour of Preston. After being impressed by the new Tom Finney Stand, Charlie then took on the great man himself in a game of table-top football and, perhaps predictably, Tom won the day 1–0 – thanks to an own goal from the king-in-waiting! Charles clearly didn't hold the defeat personally, as Tom received a richly deserved knighthood in the New Year's Honours List.

BANK BALANCE BOOSTER

Preston ended the 1970s with a cash windfall from Manchester City. The Blues purchased Michael Robinson for £765,000 in 1979 and the record fee received stood firm until 1997 when Kevin Kilbane fetched £1.25m when he moved to West Bromwich Albion. Five years later City returned to Deepdale to buy Jon Macken – and again smash the club's record fee received by coughing up £5.5m. We look forward to more of the same from City in the years to come!

PLAY ON!

In 1997 the Charter Theatre put on a play in honour of the great Tom Finney. Entitled *Legend* and staged by the Certain Curtain Theatre Group, the play was a great success – a bit like the great man himself!

THE EARLIEST HOOLIES?

Hard as it may seem to believe, hooliganism stretches back to almost when football first began. In 1885, after North End beat Aston Villa 5–0 in a friendly match, the PNE players and fans came under attack – as did Villa – as the the two teams were pelted with stones, attacked with sticks, punched, kicked and spat at. Just as well it wasn't a 0–0 draw! Disturbingly, one Preston player was beaten so severely that he lost consciousness. The following year, North Enders were caught up in violent scenes after fighting broke out with Queen's Park fans in a railway station – this is believed to be the first recorded instance of football hooliganism away from a match. In 1905, after a clash with Lancastrian rivals Blackburn Rovers, several PNE fans were tried for hooliganism, including a drunk and disorderly 70-year-old woman! In more modern times, North End have had a notorious hooligan firm known as the Preston Paras.

MAC ATTACK

During Sammy McIlroy's brief stay at Deepdale between 1989 and 1991, the former Manchester United and Northern Ireland star played a reserve game for PNE against Wigan Athletic – among the Latics' starting line up? Sammy McIlroy Junior!

MACKEN A NAME FOR HIMSELF

Former Manchester United junior Jon Macken's goal from just inside the halfway line against Manchester City in the 2001 Division One Lancashire derby earned him a £5.5m move to Kevin Keegan's side just a few months later. A novel way to send your CV to a prospective employer and a spectacular way for the Town End to celebrate its first match! The Lilywhites beat City 2–1, just for the record.

TONY ELLIS: PNE LEGEND

Position: Striker
Career at PNE: Two spells: 1987–89 and 1992–94
Apps: 176
Goals: 80

Tony Ellis had two successful stints at Deepdale before making the move to Bloomfield Road. Having failed to impress during a one-year spell at Oldham Athletic, Tony Ellis first made the move to Preston in October 1987 when then-boss John McGrath spent £23,000 on the striker. Ellis was an instant hit as he scored the winning goal in the last minute of his debut and went on to score 31 more goals for the club over two seasons.

Preston had suffered financially for a number of years and had even incorporated a plastic pitch at Deepdale in a bid to seek more revenue. So when Alan Ball's Stoke City bid £250,000 for Ellis in 1989, North End simply couldn't refuse. The striker spent three years with the Potters but suffered a number of injuries and was unable to make his mark at the Victoria Ground. As a result, the former Preston striker made his way back to Deepdale. Forward Graham Shaw was used as a makeweight in the deal, which was worth an additional £50,000. The cash-plus-player exchange deal made Ellis Preston's record signing.

Ellis' second stint saw him named the club's Player of the Year in consecutive seasons. His goalscoring ability was a constant threat to any opposition and in 1994 Ellis led his side to the play-off final. Unfortunately, this would end in defeat and Ellis would never play for the club again. He completed his controversial move to arch-rivals Blackpool after failing to agree a new deal with North End and despite rumours a year later that the striker may return yet again, this never materialised. In 2004, the former Preston favourite was inducted into the Blackpool FC Hall of Fame, just to rub salt in the wound.

LOAN RANGERS

Here are all the players who have played on loan for North End since 1970. Some (with asterisk*) went onto earn permanent deals – others either didn't impress or had served their purpose.

Loaners from 1970 to the end of the 2009/10 season:

Player	Month	From
Roger Davies	Aug 1972	Derby
Ron Healey	Dec 1973	Manchester City
Mike Elwiss *	Mar 1980	Crystal Palace
Jimmy Mullen	Nov 1981	Rotherham Utd
Martin Hodge (1st loan)	Dec 1981	Everton
Jim Arnold	Oct 1982	Everton
Martin Hodge (2nd loan)	Feb 1983	Everton
Jeff Wealands	Dec 1984	Manchester Utd
Bob Atkins *	Feb 1985	Sheffield Utd
Gary Brazil *	Feb 1985	Sheffield Utd
Bobby Cooper	Dec 1985	Leicester City

Player	Month	From
Shaun Reid	Dec 1985	Rochdale
Phil Harrington	Feb 1986	Blackpool
Simon Jeffels	Oct 1987	Barnsley
Paul Fitzpatrick	Dec 1988	Carlisle United
Nigel Jemson	Mar 1989	Nottingham Forest
Pat Scully	Sept 1989	Arsenal
Mike Stowell	Feb 1990	Everton
Greg Fee (1st loan)	Sept 1990	Sheffield Wed
Greg Fee (2nd loan)	Jan 1991	Sheffield Wed
Matt Jackson	Mar 1991	Luton Town
Paul Cross	Sept 1991	Barnsley
Julian James	Sept 1991	Luton Town
Tim Allpress	Oct 1991	Luton Town
Lenny Johnrose	Jan 1992	Blackburn Rovers
Neil Whitworth	Jan 1992	Manchester Utd
Shaun Garnett	Feb 1992	Tranmere Rovers
Deiniol Graham	Oct 1992	Barnsley
Colin Taylor	Nov 1992	Wolves
John Fowler	Feb 1993	Cambridge Utd
Stuart Rimmer	Dec 1994	Chester City
David Beckham	Feb 1995	Manchester Utd
Alan Johnson	Mar 1995	Lincoln City
Charlie Bishop	Jan 1996	Barnsley
Paul Birch	Mar 1996	Wolves
Lee Ashcroft *	Sept 1996	West Brom
Darren Patterson	Oct 1996	Luton Town
Darren Beckford	Jan 1997	Hearts
Shaun Teale	Jan 1997	Tranmere Rovers
Mark Stallard	Feb 1997	Bradford City
John Mullin	Feb 1998	Sunderland
Darren Byfield	Nov 1998	Aston Villa
Craig Harrison	Jan 1999	Middlesbrough
Steve Basham *	Feb 1999	Southampton
Andy Gray	Feb 1999	Nottingham Forest

Player	Month	From
Neil Clement	Mar 1999	Chelsea
Alex Mathie	Sept 1999	Dundee United
David Beresford	Dec 1999	Huddersfield Town
Iain Anderson *	Feb 2000	Toulouse
Brett Angell	Feb 2000	Stockport County
Brian McBride	Sept 2000	Colombus (USA)
Erik Meijer	Oct 2000	Liverpool
Richard Cresswell *	Mar 2001	Leicester City
Paul Reid	Jan 2002	Rangers
Thordur Gudjonsson	Feb 2002	Las Palmas
Colin Hendry	Feb 2002	Bolton Wanderers
Gareth Ainsworth	Mar 2002	Wimbledon
Omar Daley	Aug 2003	Reading
Claude Davis *	Aug 2003	Portmore (Jamaica)
Scott Gemmill	Mar 2004	Everton
John Curtis	Sept 2004	Portsmouth
Guylain N'Dumbu-Nsungu	Sept 2004	Sheffield Wed
Filipe Oliveira	Dec 2004	Chelsea
Rob Kozluk	Jan 2005	Sheffield Utd
Chris Day	Feb 2005	QPR
Yoann Folly	Mar 2005	Southampton
Jermal Johnson	Oct 2005	Blackburn Rovers
Brian Stock *	Jan 2006	Bournemouth
Jason Jarrett *	Mar 2006	Norwich City
Marcus Stewart	Mar 2006	Bristol City
David Jones	Aug 2006	Manchester Utd
Tommy Miller	Nov 2006	Sunderland
Frank Songo'o	Mar 2007	Portsmouth
Andy Carroll	Aug 2007	Newcastle Utd
Paul Gallagher	Aug 2007	Blackburn Rovers
John Halls	Nov 2007	Reading
Craig Beattie	Mar 2008	West Brom
Tomas Priskin	Mar 2008	Watford

Player	Month	From
Jon Parkin *	Aug 2008	Stoke City
Ross Wallace *	Aug 2008	Sunderland
Jay McEveley	Sept 2008	Derby County
Wayne Brown	Oct 2008	Hull City
Eddie Nolan *	Oct 2008	Blackburn Rovers
Andrew Davies	Feb 2009	Stoke City
Lee Williamson	Mar 2009	Watford
Neil Collins *	Sept 2009	Wolves
Michael Tongue	Nov 2009	Stoke City
Danny Welbeck	Jan 2010	Manchester Utd
Matty James	Feb 2010	Manchester Utd
Tom Williams	Feb 2010	Peterborough Utd
Elliott Ward	Mar 2010	Coventry City

JON PARKIN: PNE LEGEND

Name: Jon Parkin
Position: Striker
Years played for PNE: 2008-Present
Apps: 87
Goals: 21

A product of the Barnsley FC academy system, Jon Parkin has played for seven different clubs during his ten-year career, but finally seems to have settled as a member of Preston's Championship side. In the year 2000 alone, the English striker played for three separate clubs, having been loaned out by parent club Barnsley to both Hartlepool United and York City. Over the next six years, Parkin would play for Macclesfield Town, Hull City and Stoke City, before eventually moving to Deepdale.

In August 2008, Parkin left Stoke and signed for Preston on an emergency loan deal. The move was to become permanent only days after he initially signed as on 1 September Parkin put pen to paper for a three-year contract. One year earlier, North End had lost their prize asset, David Nugent, to then Premier League outfit Portsmouth and the Lilywhites hoped Parkin would fill the void left by the England international. It wasn't long before Parkin impressed for his new club and the striker is now affectionately known as 'The Beast'. The 6ft 4in target man has combined an array of technical ability with his sheer physical presence in order to become a regular fixture in North End's first team and a favourite among the fans.

A run of good form during the 2008/09 season saw Parkin named the club's Player of the Year and help Preston reach the Championship play-offs. It was his goal in the club's 2–1 win over QPR that booked North End's place in the top six, though the Lilywhites couldn't progress past the semi-finals. Parkin is capable of causing a problem for any defence in the division and much is expected of the striker who is expected to be the key to any promotion push that Preston seek in the future.

JON MACKEN: PNE LEGEND

Position: Striker
Career at PNE: 1997–2002
Apps: 218
Goals: 73

Popular striker Jon Macken played for the club from 1997 to 2002, during the most successful spell of his career. Having been deemed surplus to requirements at Manchester United, where he had signed a professional contract in 1996, Macken joined the Lilywhites in July 1997 in a deal worth £250,000. With 73 goals in five seasons, the striker's goalscoring ability helped North End to the Championship in 2000 and a place in the 2001 Championship play-off. Little was expected of Preston the year they were promoted to England's second tier, but Macken inspired a fourth-place finish. North End went on to reach the play-off final, after overcoming a strong Birmingham side, but were beaten convincingly by Bolton Wanderers. Despite this disappointment, Macken was named Player of the Year in 2001.

Macken's form eventually resulted in a £5.5m bid from Manchester City which was accepted. The Mancunian moved to the Premier League but failed to live up to his potential as injury disrupted his time with the Blues. Inconsistency at club level didn't stop the England under-20 international earning a full cap with the Republic of Ireland, though this would be his only appearance for his country. Eventually he was sold to Crystal Palace for a cut-price £1.1m in 2005 and hasn't returned to the Premier League since.

Now playing for League One side Walsall, the veteran Macken will be hoping to regain some of the form he once showed at Preston.

ARCHIE GEMMILL: PNE LEGEND

Position: Midfielder
Career at PNE: 1967–70
Apps: 99
Goals: 13

After plying his trade in his native Scotland for St Mirren, midfielder Archie Gemmill made the move to Deepdale for a fee of £13,000. Though he spent three years playing for Preston, it was spells at Derby County and Nottingham Forest that would make the Scot's name. Having decided to leave North End in 1970, Gemmill was faced with a choice. Either he could join league champions Everton or he could move to the Baseball Ground to play for Brian Clough's Derby County. Clough's trusted assistant Peter Taylor had spotted Gemmill's talent and while the player himself seemed unsure about a move to County, Clough was able to persuade him to resist the lure of Everton and instead sign for him. Preston earned £60,000 from the sale.

The midfielder's decision was justified at the end of the 1971/72 season when Derby County were crowned English champions. Gemmill went on to lift the trophy as captain of the Rams in 1975 when Clough led the club to a second First Division title. Upon Clough's move from Derby to Nottingham Forest, Gemmill followed. He cost Forest £25,000 in 1977 and won two League Cups and another title during his time at the club. Nine years of playing for Clough were soon to come to an end, however, after the manager dropped Gemmill from his line-up for the 1979 European Cup final. This unsettled the Scot and, after a fall-out with his boss, he moved on to Birmingham City. Though he'd never play for Clough again, Gemmill reunited with his former boss at Nottingham Forest in 1984 as a coach.

An international success also, Gemmill represented his country on 43 occasions. His most memorable moment was a goal against the Netherlands in the 1978 World Cup – a goal that is widely considered one of the competition's best ever individual efforts.

GOALSCORERS – ALL-TIME LIST

Here are the players who at least made it to 50 strikes during their North End career, led by the legend himself, Sir Tom Finney.

Tom Finney	210
Tommy Roberts	180
Alex Bruce	171
Alex Dawson	132
Tommy Thompson	128
Charlie Wayman	117
Jimmy Ross	101
Percy Smith	95
Tony Ellis	86
Steve Elliott	78
Jon Macken	74
Angus Morrison	74
Mike Elwiss	72
George Harrison	72
Jimmy Baxter	71
Gary Brazil	71
Ted Harper	69
Frank Becton	65
Bud Maxwell	65
Graham Alexander	63
Bobby Beattie	62

Richard Cresswell	58
Dennis Hatsell	58
Roland Woodhouse	58
Jimmy Dougal	57
Brian Godfrey	57
Willie McIntosh	54
Norman Robson	54
John Thomas	54
Alex James	53
Alec Reid	50

SUPER TED

Ted Harper broke all club records with his scoring exploits during the 1932/33 season, bagging 37 all told. His haul included two four-goal salvos and two hat-tricks and he also bagged three penalties – not bad from just 42 appearances in all competitions. He finished some 28 goals ahead of the next highest scorer who couldn't even break into double figures and his tally accounted for exactly half of PNE's 74 league goals that season.

OUR GRACIE'S UP FRONT!

Legendary wartime entertainer Gracie Fields kicked off a charity match at Deepdale prior to the 1934/35 campaign, much to the delight of the home support. Rumours she beat three men before deftly chipping the keeper and then running to the fans shouting 'Let's 'ave it!' are, sadly, unfounded . . .

NORTH END FAIL TO SCORE –
FOR SEVEN YEARS!

The outbreak of the Second World War in 1939 meant that just three games of the Third Division (North) 1939/40 campaign were completed before league football was indefinitely suspended. Having drawn 0–0 at home to Leeds United and Sheffield United, North End then lost 2–0 at Grimsby Town before the season was abandoned.

The next official league action wasn't until 31 August 1946 when league football resumed following the end of hostilities. With the games having to be replayed, North End went on something of a goal frenzy, beating Leeds 3–2, losing to Sheffield United 2–1 but beating Grimsby Town 3–2 at Blundell Park. For the record, Oldham were then dispatched 5–1 at Deepdale, making it twelve goals in the first four games, well and truly ending the seven-year drought!

DAVID MOYES: PNE LEGEND

Position: Centre-back
Career at PNE: 1993–9
Apps: 159
Goals: 18

Though he was never the most prominent of players, David Moyes spent six seasons on the pitch for Preston before becoming a part of the club's backroom staff. In January 1998, with Preston struggling to survive in Division Two, manager Gary Peters was sacked and Moyes was hired as his successor. This was to be the beginning of his successful managerial career. Having led his Preston side to safety in 1998, North End reached the play-off semi-finals, eventually losing out to Gillingham. One year later, Moyes' team were crowned Division Two champions and were promoted as a result. His successful spell continued in 2001 as Preston reached fourth in the league. Though enough for a play-off spot, the Lilywhites were unable to gain promotion to the Premier League via the play-offs

Despite not quite reaching the same heights in the 2001/02 season, Moyes became a much coveted manager – interesting a number of high-profile clubs. In the end it was Everton who captured the Scot's signature. After only four years at Deepdale, Moyes had transformed Preston from Division Two stragglers to Championship play-off finalists and found the offer of Premier League management too great to refuse.

Moyes' eight years as manager of Everton have been largely successful. Though never blessed with the largest transfer kitty, the manager's tactical nous and ability to spot a bargain have seen the Toffees rarely out of the top half of the table since he took over. Everton's success peaked in 2005 when Moyes led his side to fourth and qualified for the European Champions League. Backed by loyal Chairman Bill Kenwright, Moyes has continued the success that he brought to Deepdale during his time at Goodison Park and despite working on a minimal budget, the signings of Tim Cahill, Phil Jagielka and Mikel Arteta for minimal fees are testament to the Scot's all-round managerial prowess.

THE PNE PITCH

Laid: Summer 1986
Designer: En-Tout-Cas
Cost: Not documented, but QPR's synthetic pitch
           is said to have costed £300,000 at around the
           same time
Purpose: To help financially as fewer games would
           be postponed in bad weather and the club
           reached a deal with the council where the
           council would pay to use Deepdale
Result: Created closer links with schools and clubs
           who requested to use the pitch during the week

Former PNE Chairman Keith Leeming on the pitch: 'The club was on the verge of closure, but the plastic pitch was a lifeline in a very dark period in Preston's history. In my view, it was the beginning of a new era and the pitch played a very significant role in keeping the club in business.'

1986/87: John McGrath's PNE win promotion to Division Three having finished second in the league

1988: FA ban artificial turf but both PNE and Oldham continue playing on the surface

1994 (eight seasons later): Plastic pitch removed due to a Football League directive that claimed all Football League sides must play on grass before the 1995/96 season

Record on plastic:

1986/87:	W 16	D 4	L 3	F 36	A 18
1987/88:	W 10	D 6	L 7	F 30	A 23
1988/89:	W 14	D 7	L 2	F 56	A 31
1989/90:	W 10	D 7	L 6	F 42	A 30

1990/91:	W 11	D 5	L 7	F 33	A 29
1991/92:	W 12	D 7	L 4	F 42	A 32
1992/93:	W 8	D 5	L 10	F 41	A 47
1993/94:	W 13	D 5	L 3	F 46	A 23
P 182	W 94	D 46	L 42	F 326	A 233

Win ratio: 51 per cent

TOM'S RIGHT AT HOME ...

Tom Finney was inducted into the National Football Museum's inaugural Hall of Fame at Deepdale – here are the other inductees from the 2002 launch:

Gordon Banks
George Best
Eric Cantona
'Dixie' Dean
John Charles
Sir Bobby Charlton
Kenny Dalglish
Peter Doherty
Paul Gascoigne
Duncan Edwards
Jimmy Greaves
Johnny Haynes
Kevin Keegan
Bryan Robson
Denis Law
Nat Lofthouse
Billy Wright
Sir Stanley Matthews
Peter Shilton
Bobby Moore
Dave Mackay

Women's Inductee
Lily Parr

Managers
Sir Matt Busby
Brian Clough
Sir Alex Ferguson
Bob Paisley
Sir Alf Ramsey
Bill Shankly

NOW THAT'S A COMEBACK!

One of North End's greatest comebacks has to be the October 1932 recovery away to Grimsby Town. The Lilywhites found themselves 4–0 down after 13 minutes – all goals scored by Glover – but fought back to 4–4 before conceding a later fifth to the Mariners. The efforts weren't in vain, however, as a late equaliser made it 5–5 and PNE returned to Lancashire with a very well-earned point.

HAT-TRICK HEROES

Here is a complete list of all the players who got to keep the match ball during their North End careers...

Jimmy Ross	6/10/1888	Stoke	H
John Goddall	27/10/1888	Wolves	H
Jack Gordon	3/11/1888	Notts County	A
John Goddall	3/11/1888	Notts County	A
Nick Ross	14/9/1889	Stoke	H
Nick Ross	28/9/1889	Burnley	A
Jimmy Ross	28/9/1889	West Brom	H
Nick Ross	12/10/1889	Bolton Wanderers	A
Nick Ross	25/12/1889	Aston Villa	H
Nick Ross	11/1/1890	Derby County	H
Georgie Drummond	18/1/1890	Newton Heath	H
Georgie Drummond	12/12/1891	Notts County	H
David Russell	22/10/1892	Aston Villa	H
Jimmy Ross	14/1/1893	Sheffield Wed	A
Jimmy Ross	21/1/1893	Burton Swifts	H
Frank Becton	21/1/1893	Burton Swift	H
Frank Becton	25/2/1893	M'boro Ironopolis	H
Frank Becton	31/3/1893	Notts County	H

Frank Becton	10/4/1893	Wolves	H
Jimmy Ross	23/9/1893	Darwen	H
Jack Barton	27/1/1894	Reading	H
John Cowan	27/1/1894	Reading	H
Jimmy Ross	27/1/1894	Reading	H
Frank Becton	27/1/1894	Reading	H
Jimmy Ross	3/3/1894	West Brom	H
Frank Becton	5/1/1895	West Brom	A
Tom Pratt	28/1/1899	Grimsby Town	H
Jackie Pierce	4/11/1899	Notts County	H
George Henderson	3/2/1900	West Brom	H
Andrew Gara	21/9/1901	Barnsley	A
Dick Pegg	28/12/1901	Lincoln City	H
Tom Pratt	29/03/1902	Stockport County	H
Percy Smith	28/2/1903	Port Vale	H
Percy Smith	13/2/1904	Leicester Fosse	A
Percy Smith	3/9/1904	Sunderland	H
Percy Smith	11/2/1905	Notts County	A
Dickie Bond	21/4/1905	Sheffield Utd	H
Charles Dawson	7/9/1908	Chelsea	H
Jonathan Morley	1/1/1913	Glossop NE	A
Fred Osborn	29/11/1913	Middlesbrough	H
Fred Osborn	10/1/1914	Bristol Rovers	H
Fred Osborn	17/1/1914	Sheffield Wed	H
Rowland Woodhouse	27/12/1920	Blackburn Rovers	H
Tommy Roberts	29/1/1921	Watford	H
Tommy Roberts	19/2/1921	Luton	A
Tommy Roberts	26/3/1921	West Brom	A
Tommy Roberts	3/9/1921	Bolton Wanderers	H
Rowland Woodhouse	5/11/1921	Burnley	A
Fred Marquis	6/1/1923	Aston Villa	H
Tommy Roberts	8/2/1923	Stoke City	H
James Ferris	5/1/1924	Burnley	H
Rowland Woodhouse	10/1/1925	Manchester City	H
Walter Jackson	12/12/1925	Clapham Orient	H

Tommy Roberts	8/1/1927	Lincoln City	A
George Harrison	29/8/1927	Hull City	H
Tommy Roberts	26/11/1927	Notts County	H
Norman Robson	21/1/1928	Wolves	H
Ken Cameron	5/5/1928	Grimsby Town	A
Norman Robson	27/8/1928	Reading	H
George Harrison	3/11/1928	Grimsby Town	H
Sandy Hair	17/11/1928	Clapham Orient	H
Alex Reid	23/2/1929	Port Vale	H
Bobby Crawford	21/9/1929	Stoke City	H
James McClelland	6/9/1930	Reading	A
Tom Scott	4/10/1930	Millwall	A
George Bargh	13/12/1930	Cardiff City	H
Vincent Farrell	17/3/1931	Charlton Athletic	H
Ted Harper	16/1/1932	Southampton	A
Ted Harper	6/2/1932	Wolves	H
Dick Rowley	16/4/1932	Notts County	A
Ted Harper	23/4/1932	Plymouth Argyle	H
Ted Harper	29/8/1932	Burnley	H
Ted Harper	22/10/1932	West Ham Utd	H
Ted Harper	11/2/1933	Manchester Utd	H
Ted Harper	11/3/1933	Lincoln City	H
George Stephenson	23/12/1933	Southampton	H
Jack Palethorne	17/2/1934	Northampton Town	H
George Bargh	31/3/1934	Millwall	H
Bud Maxwell	19/1/1935	Huddersfield Town	A
Bud Maxwell	13/4/1935	Stoke City	H
Bud Maxwell	5/12/1936	West Brom	H
Frank O'Donnell	30/1/1937	Stoke City	H
Frank O'Donnell	20/2/1937	Exeter City	H
Bud Maxwell	11/9/1937	Liverpool	H
Frank O'Donnell	8/1/1937	West Ham Utd	H
Willie McIntosh	7/9/1946	Grimsby Town	A
Willie McIntosh	14/9/1946	Charlton Athletic	H
Bobbie Beattie	4/9/1948	Middlesbrough	H

Charlie Wayman	25/12/1950	QPR	A
Charlie Wayman	20/1/1951	Grimsby Town	A
Ken Horton	10/3/1951	Barnsley	H
Charlie Wayman	16/2/1952	Arsenal	A
Charlie Wayman	3/1/1953	Middlesbrough	H
Charlie Wayman	10/1/1953	Wolves	H
Bobby Foster	22/8/1953	Middlesbrough	A
Jimmy Baxter	26/8/1953	Sheffield Utd	H
Charlie Wayman	24/9/1953	Sunderland	H
Dennis Hatsell	19/4/1954	Tottenham Hotspur	A
Charlie Wayman	21/8/1954	Manchester City	H
Peter Higham	30/10/1954	Sheffield Wed	H
Ken Waterhouse	30/4/1955	Charlton Athletic	A
Tommy Thompson	3/11/1956	Sunderland	H
Sammy Taylor	2/2/1957	Portsmouth	H
Sammy Taylor	28/9/1957	Chelsea	H
Tommy Thompson	1/2/1958	Birmingham City	H
Sammy Taylor	1/2/1958	Birmingham City	H
Tommy Thompson	19/12/1959	Chelsea	H
Alfie Biggs	2/12/1961	Scunthorpe & L Utd	H
Alfie Biggs	14/4/1962	Brighton & H A	H
Alex Dawson	15/4/1963	Swansea Town	H
Alex Dawson	31/8/1963	Swansea Town	H
Alex Ashworth	7/12/1963	Bury	H
Dave Wilson	26/12/1963	Cardiff City	A
Brian Godfrey	29/8/1964	Ipswich Town	A
Alex Dawson	14/11/1964	Charlton Athletic	A
Alex Dawson	13/3/1965	Portsmouth	H
Alex Dawson	20/3/1965	Manchester City	A
Brian Greenhalgh	16/3/1966	Bolton Wanderers	A
Ernie Hannigan	7/5/1966	Cardiff City	H
Brian Godfrey	7/5/1966	Cardiff City	H
Willie Irvine	23/3/1968	Huddersfield Town	H
Gerry Ingram	12/9/1970	Reading	H
Mel Holden	26/11/1974	Blyth Spartans	H

Alex Bruce	12/10/1976	Peterborough Utd	H
Alex Bruce	28/2/1978	Colchester Utd	H
Steve Elliott	28/8/1982	Millwall	H
Steve Elliott	27/12/1983	Scunthorpe Utd	A
Steve Elliott	22/2/1984	Rochdale	A
John Thomas	16/9/1986	Halifax Town	H
John Thomas	15/11/1986	Bury	H
John Thomas	9/12/1986	Chorley	H
Gary Brazil	25/10/1988	Gillingham	H
Tony Ellis	25/2/1989	Chesterfield	H
Graham Shaw	22/8/1989	Tranmere Rovers	H
Brian Mooney	23/9/1989	Chester City	H
Steve Harper	24/2/1990	Cardiff City	H
Ronnie Jepson	19/2/1991	Burnley	H
Tony Ellis	10/10/1992	Blackpool	A
Tony Ellis	27/3/1993	Rotherham Utd	H
Mike Conroy	28/8/1993	Shrewsbury Town	H
Tony Ellis	9/10/1993	Chesterfield	H
Andy Saville	21/10/1994	Mansfield Town	H
Steve Wilkinson	21/10/1994	Mansfield Town	H
Andy Saville	4/11/1994	Leyton Orient	H
Steve Wilkinson	20/8/1996	Wigan Athletic	A
David Reeves	16/11/1996	Altrincham	H
Lee Ashcroft	29/11/1997	Fulham	H
Bjarki Gunnlaugsson	7/12/1999	Wrexham	H
Jon Macken	5/9/2000	Shrewsbury Town	H
David Healy	3/11/2001	Stockport County	H
Ricardo Fuller	20/12/2003	Burnley	H
Richard Cresswell	4/10/2004	Leicester City	A
Richard Cresswell	1/1/2005	Sunderland	H
Jon Parkin	2/1/2010	Colchester Utd	H

PNE LEGEND: TOMMY DOCHERTY

Position: Defender
Career at PNE: 1949–58
Apps: 323
Goals: 5

A player for non-league Shettleston Juniors, Tommy Docherty was called up to National Service in 1946. Here, Docherty represented the British Army and impressed boyhood club Celtic. In 1947, 'The Doc', as he would later become affectionately known among fans, put pen to paper on a deal that would see him play for the Glasgow giants. Despite being a part of the club's Glasgow Cup winning side of 1949, Docherty was unable to become a first-team regular for the club and so moved to Deepdale that same summer. It took Docherty only two seasons to win the Second Division Championship with North End and in doing so, the club gained promotion to the top flight of English football where the club remained throughout Docherty's time at Deepdale.

Twice finishing runner-up in 1953 and 1958 would be as good as it got for Docherty, who never laid hands on the First Division title. He experienced further bittersweet emotion with the Lancashire club in 1954, when the Lilywhites were beaten at Wembley in the FA Cup final. The Scot's form for North End saw him become a regular with his national side and it was a clash between his domestic and international duties that brought an end to his time at Deepdale. Having been called upon to represent Scotland in the 1958 World Cup, Docherty ignored Preston's pleas not to go and was sold later that summer to Arsenal as a result.

Docherty wound down his career with Chelsea before moving to Australia on loan with Sydney Prague. During his time at Chelsea, the defender made the move into management as he was offered the chance to take the reins while also continuing his playing career. He would go on to manage thirteen club sides, returning to manage Preston in 1981 for a largely disastrous one-year spell.

INTERNATIONAL NORTH ENDERS

Here is a record of all the players who represented their country while playing for PNE – all records are up to date up to 1 June 2010, in date order and includes all nations.

England

W.C. Rose	1 cap	1886	
F. Dewhurst	9 caps	1886–9	11 goals
R. Howarth	4 caps	1887–91	
J. Goodall	4 caps	1888–9	3 goals
R. Holmes	7 caps	1888–95	
F. Becton	1 cap	1895	2 goals
R. Bond	5 caps	1905–6	2 goals
J. McCall	5 caps	1913–21	1 goal
A. Rawlings	1 cap	1921	
W. T Roberts	2 caps	1924	2 goals
H. Holdcroft	2 caps	1937	
T. Finney	76 caps	1946–58	30 goals
T. Thompson	1 cap	1957	
D. Nugent	1 cap	2007	1 goal

Scotland

P. McBride	6 caps	1904–9	
A. James	4 caps	1926–9	2 goals
F. O'Donnell	4 caps	1937–8	2 goals
A. Beattie	7 caps	1937–9	
G. Mutch	1 cap	1938	

T. Smith	1 cap	1938	
W. Shankly	5 caps	1938–9	
R. Beattie	1 cap	1939	
J. Dougal	1 cap	1939	1 goal
A. McLaren	3 caps	1947	4 goals
T. Docherty	22 caps	1952–8	1 goal
W. Cunningham	8 caps	1954–5	
G. Alexander	30 caps	2002–7	
B. O'Neil	1 cap	2005	
C. Davidson	2 caps	2009	
R. Wallace	1 cap	2009	

Wales

Dr Mills-Roberts	2 caps	1888	
J. Trainer	19 caps	1888–9	
R. Roberts	1 cap	1892	
S. Davies	3 caps	1920	3 goals
R. John	2 caps	1935	
B. Godfrey	3 caps	1964–5	2 goals

Northern Ireland

A. Gara	3 caps	1902	3 goals
J. Mcknight	1 cap	1912	1 goal
W. Irvine	3 caps	1968–9	2 goals
C. Murdock	17 caps	2000–2	
D. Healy	32 caps	2001–4	11 goals
A. Smith	7 caps	2004–5	

Republic of Ireland

F. O'Farrell	2 caps	1957–9	
J. O'Neill	1 cap	1960	
J. Fullam	1 cap	1960	
A. Kelly	45 caps	1962–73	
R. Tracey	8 caps	1974–6	1 goal

M. Lawrenson	1 cap	1977	
P. McGee	6 caps	1979–80	2 goals
J. Anderson	5 caps	1979	
S. St. Ledger-Hall	7 caps	2009–10	
E. Nolan	2 caps	2009	

Finland

| T. Moilanen | 3 caps | 1997–2000 | |

Iceland

| B. Gunnlaugsson | 2 caps | 2000 | 1 goal |

Jamaica

R. Fuller	10 caps	2002–4	2 goals
C. Davis	16 caps	2003–6	
O. Daley	3 caps	2005	

(while on loan from Portmore United)

Macedonia

| V. Shumulikoski | 2 caps | 2009 | |

South Africa

| G. Koumantarakis | 1 cap | 2003 | |

USA

| B. McBride | 2 caps | 2001 | 1 goal |

(while on loan from Columbus Crew)

| E. Lewis | 21 caps | 2003–5 | 5 goals |

SEASICK

Rarely have North End gone into the summer break with a more galling result than the last game of the 1947/48 season against Blackpool. After winning the bragging rights of the M55 derby with a 1–0 win at Bloomfield

Road the previous December, a crowd of 26,610 gathered at Deepdale to see what they hoped would be the completion of the league double. Instead, it was the stuff of nightmares as the Seasiders racked up seven goals without reply in a shocking afternoon.

DREAM DEBUTS

It's the start you hope for – your first game for North End, the ball comes across and you smack it home before running off to celebrate with a legion of new fans. It has happened more often than you might think – so much, that we will show you the post-war debut scores only:

Tom Finney	31/8/1946	Leeds Utd	H	3–2
Willie McIntosh	31/8/1946	Leeds Utd	H	3–2
Albert Dainty	4/1/1947	Grimsby Town	H	3–0
John Wilson	22/2/1947	Sheffield Wed	A	2–0
Harry Jackson	26/12/1947	Burnley	H	3–2
Jackie Knight	4/12/1948	Bolton Wanderers	A	3–5
Sammy Baird	27/11/1954	Sunderland	H	3–1
Tommy Thompson	20/8/1955	Everton	A	4–0
Eddie Lewis	10/12/1955	Aston Villa	A	2–3
Frank O'Farrell	1/12/1956	Man City	H	3–1
Derek Mayers	14/9/1957	Tottenham	H	3–1
Alan Spavin	30/10/1960	Arsenal	H	2–0
Alex Dawson	28/10/1961	Rotherham Utd	A	2–2
Jim Forrest	18/3/1967	Derby County	H	2–0
Archie Gemmill	23/8/1967	Norwich City	A	3–1
William Temple	23/9/1967	Plymouth Argyle	A	2–1
Bobby Ham	31/10/1970	Plymouth Argyle	A	1–1
Mike Elwiss	2/3/1974	Carlisle Utd	A	2–2
Ian Cochrane	14/5/1977	Shrewsbury Town	A	2–1
Mark Walsh	29/8/1981	Millwall	A	1–2

Paul Wilkins	25/8/1984	Doncaster Rovers	H	2–0
Simon Gibson	15/12/1984	Brentford	H	1–1
John Thomas	17/8/1985	Peterborough Utd	H	2–4
Tony Ellis	10/10/1987	Port Vale	H	3–2
Neil Williams	27/8/1988	Port Vale	H	1–3
Paul Shaw	19/4/1989	Rotherham Utd	A	1–3
Mickey Norbury	28/12/1992	Exeter City	H	2–2
Liam Watson	6/4/1993	Port Vale	A	2–2
Graeme Atkinson	15/10/1994	Hartlepool Utd	A	1–3
David Beckham	4/3/1995	Doncaster Rovers	H	2–2
Matt Carmichael	18/3/1995	Bury	H	5–0
Andy Saville	12/8/1995	Lincoln City	H	1–2
Gary Bennett	30/3/1996	Scarborough	A	2–1
Tony Lormor	8/11/1997	Luton Town	A	3–1
Darren Byfield	7/11/1998	Burnley	H	4–1
David Healy	30/12/2000	Sheffield Utd	A	2–3
Richard Cresswell	4/3/2001	Wolves	H	2–0
Mark Reid	5/2/2002	Sheffield Wed	H	4–2
Ricardo Fuller	10/8/2002	Crystal Palace	H	1–2
Brett Ormerod	31/1/2006	Crystal Palace	H	2–0
Pavel Pergl	20/2/2007	Norwich City	H	2–1
Matty James	9/2/2010	Sheffield Utd	H	2–1

CHRISTMAS CRACKERS

Between 1888 and 1958, North End regularly played a league match on Christmas Day. The festive fixture was a popular day on the footballing calendar and the Lilywhites have fared OK historically. The last game in 1958 – a 4–2 defeat at Blackpool – proved to be the straw that broke the camel's back and no more games were played on 25 December. The complete record is:

P: 40   W: 14   D: 11   L: 15   F: 73   A: 78

BOXING CLEVER?

The Boxing Day fixture remains one of the most well-attended dates in English football with bumper crowds (most of them probably eager to escape repeats on TV and turkey leftovers). Here is North End's complete record from 1888 to the 2009:

P: 82   W: 39   D: 23   L: 20   F: 137   A: 113

QUOTE/UNQUOTE: BRIAN MOONEY

'I've got lots of fond memories of my time at Preston and I particularly enjoyed playing on the plastic pitch there.'

'It was a great honour for me to be even mentioned in the same vein as Sir Tom, but there must have been a certain vintage of fans who were voting in that poll so for me to come second is an honour.'

ONE-MATCH WONDERS

For whatever reason, some players only ever managed to pull on the white shirt on one occasion. The majority in this list will claim they never had a chance – others will say that one chance was more than enough! Here, then, from most recent to oldest, are the one-game wonders:

10/4/2010	Adam Barton
2/2/2010	Jamie Proctor
18/2/2005	Chris Neal
13/11/2004	Kelvin Langmead
21/4/2003	John Anthony Kenneth Bailey

5/2/2002	Paul Mark Reid
22/8/2000	Paul Morgan
19/1/1999	Stuart King
16/3/1996	Tony Grant
12/3/1994	Farrell Noel Kilbane
25/9/1993	Lee Bamber
6/4/1993	Craig Allardyce
18/12/1992	Craig Moylon
12/12/1992	Barry Siddall
10/4/1990	Steven Anderton
22/8/1989	Andy Gill
27/10/1987	Gary Walker
3/10/1987	Simon Jeffels
5/1/1987	Paul Booth
16/12/1986	Shane Beeby
3/5/1986	Danny Ibbotson
3/5/1986	Andy Pilling
5/11/1985	Mark Rodgers
5/11/1985	Mel Tottoh
24/4/1984	Stuart John Cameron
28/11/1981	Jimmy Mullen
15/9/1981	Jimmy Bell
15/8/1978	John Kilner
8/12/1973	Gary Hudson
1/5/1972	Jim Blyth
7/12/1968	David Bright
3/9/1963	Kit Napier
23/10/1954	Tommy Lawrenson
4/1/1947	Albert Dainty
6/5/1939	David Williacy
21/2/1934	Tommy Pritchard
25/12/1933	Ted Common
15/4/1933	George Akers
28/1/1933	Harry Joseph Jones
22/2/1930	Jimmy Foster

21/4/1928	John Parry
10/9/1927	William Pilkington
2/4/1926	David McEachran
19/12/1925	Bill Bradford
31/8/1925	David Daniel
6/12/1924	Charles Henry Thompson
15/9/1924	Francis Pickering
15/9/1923	Harold Reay
23/12/1922	John Storey
31/12/1921	Nicholas Latham
7/5/1921	Thomas (Toby) Green
7/9/1914	George Dexter
25/4/1914	John Bond
13/12/1913	Frank Shanley
29/11/1913	Simeon Vickers
6/1/1912	Sid Beaumont
3/12/1910	Thomas J. Dickinson
10/9/1910	Lauchlan McLean
2/1/1908	John Donaldson
14/12/1907	Charles Williamson
9/11/1907	William J. McLaughlin
16/4/1906	William J. Blyth
29/11/1902	James Shorrock
16/4/1897	Harry Vickers
19/10/1895	William Brown
3/3/1894	James Roy
18/1/1894	E.A. Connor
12/3/1892	Tinsley Lindley
5/3/1892	John S. Taylor
6/2/1891	Archibald Pinnell
24/1/1891	Thomas Metcalfe
6/10/1888	Richard Whittle

JUST FOR THE RECORD...

Here, at a glance, is North End's records section, so next time the Lilywhites go on a 20-match winning streak, all you have to do is casually glance at this back section to discover if it's a new record or not. If it is, scribble one of these out and put the new stat in!

League
Highest Scoring Win:
Millwall 5–7 Preston North End 4/10/1930

Highest Scoring Loss:
Bradford P A 7–2 Preston North End 27/10/1928

Highest Winning Margin:
Preston North End 10–0 Stoke City 14/9/1889

Highest Losing Margin (home):
Preston North End 0–7 Blackpool 1/5/1948

Highest Losing Margin (away):
Nottm Forest 7–0 Preston North End 9/4/1927

Highest Scoring Draw:
Grimsby Town 5–5 Preston North End 15/10/1932

Cup (FA and League Cup)
Highest Scoring Win:
Preston North End 26–0 Hyde 15/10/1887

Highest Scoring Loss:
Walsall 7–3 Preston North End 16/11/1985

Highest Winning Margin:
Preston North End 26–0 Hyde 15/10/1887

Highest Losing Margin:
Charlton Athletic 6–0 Preston North End 14/2/1946
Blackburn Rovers 6–0 Preston North End 17/9/1997

Highest Scoring Draw:
Preston North End 4–4 Wigan Athletic 3/9/1996

League Sequences
Consecutive wins: 14 (25/12/1950 to 27/3/1951)

Consecutive draws: 6 (24/2/1979 to 20/3/1979)

Consecutive losses: 8 (1/10/1983 to 5/11/1983 and
    22/9/1984 to 27/10/1984)

Consecutive clean sheets: 6 (14/9/1901 to 19/10/1901 and
    9/9/1972 to 30/9/1972 and 25/3/2000 to 22/4/2000)

Games without scoring: 6 (8/4/1897 to 1/9/1897 and
    19/11/1960 to 26/12/1960)

Games without a win: 15 (14/4/1923 to 20/10/1923)

Games without a draw: 27 (24/10/1891 to 22/10/1892
    and 8/10/1958 to 4/4/1959)

Games without a loss: 23 (8/9/1888 to 14/9/1889)

Games without a clean sheet: 26 (11/10/1969 to
    31/3/1970)

Games without failing to score: 30 (15/11/1952 to
    26/8/1953)

Squad Records
Highest League Scorer in Season:
Ted Harper, 37, Division Two, 1932/33

Most League Goals in Total: Tom Finney, 187, 1946–60

Most Capped Player: Tom Finney, 76, England

Most League Appearances: Alan Kelly, 447, 1961–75

Youngest League Player: Steve Doyle, 16 years 166 days
v Tranmere Rovers, 15 November 1974

Record Transfer Fee Received: £6,000,000 for
David Nugent from Portsmouth, July 2007

Record Transfer Fee Paid: £1,500,000 for David Healy
from Manchester United, December 2000

PNE HONOURS

Division One Champions: 1888/89, 1889/90

Division One Runners-Up: 1890/91, 1891/92, 1892/93,
1905/06, 1952/53, 1957/58

Division Two Champions: 1903/04, 1912/13, 1950/51,
1999/2000

Division Two Runners-Up: 1914/15, 1933/34

Division Three Champions: 1970/71, 1995/96

Division Four Runners-Up: 1986/87

FA Cup Winners: 1889, 1938

FA Cup Runners-Up: 1888, 1922, 1937, 1954, 1964